ALL OVER THE PLACE

ALL OVER THE PLACE

ADVENTURES IN TRAVEL, TRUE LOVE, AND PETTY THEFT

GERALDINE DERUITER

PUBLICAFFAIRS
NEW YORK

PublicAffairs books are available at special discounts for bulk purchases in the
U.S. by corporations, institutions, and other organizations. For more information, please contact the Special Markets Department at Perseus Books, 2300
Chestnut Street, Suite 200, Philadelphia, PA 19103, call
(800) 810-4145, ext. 5000, or e-mail special.markets@perseusbooks.com.

Brief sections in Chapter 10 are reprinted from the author's blog.

Book Design by Amy Quinn

Library of Congress Cataloging-in-Publication Data

Names: DeRuiter, Geraldine, author.
Title: All over the place : adventures in travel, true love, and petty theft
/ Geraldine DeRuiter.
Description: First edition. | New York : PublicAffairs, [2017] | Includes
bibliographical references and index.
Identifiers: LCCN 2016042568 (print) | LCCN 2017000532 (ebook) | ISBN
9781610397636 (hardcover) | ISBN 9781610397643 (e-book) | ISBN
9781610397643 (ebook)
Subjects: LCSH: DeRuiter, Geraldine—Travel. | Adventure and
Adventurers—United States—Biography. | Bloggers—United
States—Biography.
Classification: LCC G226.D47 A3 2017 (print) | LCC G226.D47 (ebook) |
DDC 910.4—dc23
LC record available at https://lccn.loc.gov/2016042568

First Edition

LSC-C

· 10 9 8 7 6 5 4 3 2

For the love of my life.*

*I'm obviously referring to my husband, Rand. Unless Jeff Goldblum is reading this, in which case, Jeff, I'm talking about you.

CONTENTS

A DISCLAIMER

THE PROBLEM WITH WRITING A book ostensibly about travel is that people automatically assume it falls into one of two categories:

1. It is somehow informative.
2. It involves a button-nosed protagonist nursing a broken heart who, rather than watching *The Princess Bride* while eating an entire five-gallon vat of ice cream directly out of the container while weeping (like a normal person), instead decides to travel the world, inevitably falling for some chiseled stranger with bulging pectoral muscles and a disdain for wearing clothing above the waist.

Let me disabuse you of each of these notions immediately.

First, this book will likely teach you very little about the places mentioned herein. Despite having spent the last half decade in the state of transient unemployment known as travel blogging, I am woefully unqualified to provide any useful information in that regard.

I cannot tell you how to find the best restaurant in Rome or where to get the best rate on plane tickets, nor can I provide any historical context for a single geographic location without wandering into the fictional and oddly perverse. (Did you know that the Washington Monument was built to subtly ridicule our first president's shockingly angular wang? I have never been to the Leaning Tower of Pisa, which is probably for the best.)

There are plenty of travel writers and personalities who have covered all those important topics in the travel realm far better than I could (even if I *were* sober, and not drunk on sugar and the intoxicating power of having one's own blog, as I usually am). They even cite reputable sources beyond "the Internet" and "I think I saw it on *Jeopardy* one time" and "Shut up, dickface, it's totally true."

If that is what you are seeking, I recommend the work of the inimitable Rick Steves, the apotheosis of all travel writers.

Steves has made a career of helping the hapless travel the world, and his guides are useful if you actually want to know something about planning a trip or finding your way through a foreign country.

I feel that I must take a moment here to say that while I respect him for his travel prowess and will begrudgingly admit to even having benefited from it on occasion, I am automatically disdainful of people who know what they are talking about (mostly because I so rarely do). Consequently, I have described Steves as "a human turnip," "John Denver minus the sex appeal," and "a toe with glasses." (I know these are unkind things to say, and insulting someone based on their appearance is wrong. By way of explanation, I'm kind of a horrible person.) I might also be slightly jealous of his sheer popularity. Not to mention, this is a man who named his book series *Europe Through the Back Door* and then didn't even have the decency to make them the least bit pornographic. I just can't condone that sort of wasted opportunity.

Second, while most travel memoirs would dictate that I find love somewhere along the way, that was not the case for me. I met the love of my life long before this story began, on the bastion of romance that is King County Metro's 43 bus, under flickering fluorescent lights, surrounded by drunk college kids. As one does.

And I do not think one could call the love of my life chiseled. But he has twinkly eyes and puts up with my insufferable jokes, and he makes a good schnitzel. (That's not a euphemism or anything. He really makes a good schnitzel.)

Also, my nose would never, *ever* be described as button-like.

So if this book by a travel writer is not about travel or about finding romance somewhere along the road, then where does that leave us? These last six years have taught me a great number of things, though being able to read a map is not one of them. I still have only a vague understanding of where Russia is, but I understand my Russian father better now than I ever have before. I have learned that at least half of what I thought was my mother's functional insanity was actually an equally incurable condition called "being Italian." I have learned about my family and myself, about brain tumors and lost jobs and lost luggage and lost opportunities and just getting lost, in countless terminals and cabs and hotel lobbies across the globe.

And I've learned what it's like to travel the world with someone you already know and love. How they help you make sense of things and can, by some sort of alchemy I still don't quite understand, make foreign cities and far-off places feel like home. How days roll into weeks and months and years, and during that time you will fight and scream and laugh and cry with them, possibly all at once. That you can see so much of the world, and realize it is far bigger than the two of you, and still somehow feel that your love, squishy and imperfect and mortal, might be a story worth telling.

So, if there is any advice I could dispense, it would be this: it's absolutely incredible, the things you can learn from not having a clue about where you're going—lessons that emerge after making a wrong turn, or saying the wrong thing, or even after accidentally doing something right. And in my case, this was all undertaken not in the company of a new love, but one that has enough miles on it to circle the earth three, maybe four times, is now sufficiently jet lagged, and lost its pants somewhere over Greenland.

I offer these minor epiphanies to you with the caveat that you shouldn't try to replicate the circumstances that led to them. Learn from my mistakes, but do not repeat them. Doing the latter will almost certainly result in unintended consequences, in particular petty theft, destruction of private property, low-blood-sugar-induced screaming, and flooding a boutique hotel room in New York City with a deluge of putrescence so heinous you will consider crafting a new identity to escape it.

But most notably, if you follow my lead, you will get hopelessly, miserably lost. As in, "I may have just crossed over an international border without realizing it" lost, or "I have never seen any of this before and supposedly this is my hometown" lost, or that panicky "I think I accidentally entered a magic realm via a portal in the back of a wardrobe" sort of lost.

That said, as I've learned, getting lost isn't the worst thing in the world. If you are trying to find yourself, it's a great place to start.

1

GELATO IS AN EXCELLENT SUBSTANCE IN WHICH TO DROWN YOUR SORROWS

IF THE MANY TIMES THAT I'd been dumped were any indication, I was not going to handle losing my job well.

Blessed with this knowledge, and that of the many red flags signaling the impending end to my employment, I preemptively went into breakup mode. I figured I needed plenty of alcohol, sugar, and carbohydrates at close proximity. So, in a shocking display of fiscal irresponsibility from someone for whom unemployment was imminent, I decided to go to Italy. I reasoned the country had seen its share of ugly endings: that whole mess with Caesar in the Senate, the fall of the Holy Roman Empire, the final scene of *The Godfather, Part III*—so it could handle mine. Plus, I wasn't sure if they would pay me for the vacation time I still had left.

It was early 2008. America was about to enter its worst financial crisis since the Great Depression: 2.6 million people lost their jobs that year, and I was about to become one of them.

✳ ✳ ✳

MINE WAS A DEVIATION FROM how most travel stories begin. The path for the modern wanderer always seems to follow the same course—one that traces through Southeast Asia, involves at least three life-changing epiphanies vaguely invoking Buddhism, and necessitates wearing those pants with the zip-off legs. And the starting point is invariably this: they quit. They voluntarily cast off those miserable shackles of stable employment; they spin the globe and pick a spot at random. *There. I shall go there.*

And to their credit, this tactic works if you are young, debt-free, and willing to accept Anthony Bourdain as your lord and savior.

Personally, I've never understood quitting a stable job in order to see the world. I'd put it in the same mental file in which I've placed "eating cake for every meal" and "sex with Jeff Goldblum circa *Jurassic Park*." That is, things that are fun to think about but impossible or irresponsible in practice, due to the constraints of space-time, existing restraining orders, and the limitations of the human pancreas.

"Life is too short to spend behind a desk," says every damn job-quitting travel writer, ever. But I'd argue that, statistically speaking, life gets a hell of a lot shorter without health insurance or a steady income.

Not to mention, whenever I've spun a globe and tried to pinpoint a destination, my finger always ends up in the middle of the Pacific, adrift, surrounded by thousands of miles of blue enamel paint in every direction. (I try not to extract too much symbolism from this.)

I am not impulsive. I do not like spontaneity. I like order and predictability, and I want to immediately know whether or not the protagonist lives until the end of the story.

Whenever people ask about how all this started, I am very clear about one thing: I did not quit.

I was laid off.

∗ ∗ ∗

I AM A RARE BREED—like morning people or children who enjoy visiting the dentist or vegans who aren't self-righteous—I liked my job. My coworkers were funny and brilliant and caring, the sort who could make a deadline with time to spare and drive you home in rush hour traffic that one time you got food poisoning, simultaneously screaming at someone for cutting them off while patting your back as you threw up.

In the years since the small board game company I worked for folded, my former colleagues have gone on to do amazing things. They've started their own successful, award-winning companies. They've served as musical directors for nationally renowned productions. The driver who deftly navigated Seattle traffic while I barfed repeatedly into a bag went on to write and illustrate numerous award-winning children's books. And to this day, he's never, ever held that vomitous afternoon against me, though I hold hope it will one day be fodder for a rather amazing pop-up picture book.

They would fan out across the country and the world, lighting up dark offices and stale conference rooms with their talent. But for a little while we'd been together, shining in one place—chasing one another around the office in absurd Halloween costumes. Taking trips to toy stores in the name of research. Working on a product for so many hours straight that we were rendered tired and giggly.

"Someone give me a tagline for this game in under five words!" I once yelled to no one in particular.

"CHOKE SAFE!" someone shouted in reply.

We felt invincible and suffered the obligatory punishment for our hubris. Ultimately, we were powerless in the matter—as editors, designers, and marketers, we had no control over the swift expansion into other media that caused the company to lose millions within the span of a few months.

We knew it was a fire sale, regardless of all the interviews our charismatic CEO had given about how this was his triumph. The spring of 2007 had already brought one round of lay-offs, and the rest of us felt like we were on borrowed time. Christmas was marked by a lack of end-of-the-year bonuses, and soon after we got the news that our stock was worthless.

✳ ✳ ✳

THE TRIP TO ITALY HAD been my friend Kati's idea, discussed the previous summer as a means of breaking up the months of steady rain and gray skies that characterized every month in Seattle that wasn't August. It began purely as a joke over Gchat, one that grew and caught us up in it so that there was no turning back. We simply had to nod and go with it, like the sartorial rise of trucker hats or the return of the mustache. By the time you realize what's going on, it's too late: you've already decided to book round-trip tickets to Rome, and every guy at your local bar looks like Ashton Kutcher, circa 2005.

Kati, like me, had Italian ancestry and a decent understanding of the language (her grammar was significantly better than mine, but I grew up screaming it fluently at my relatives over a kitchen table). She'd spent a semester in Italy years ago and wanted to go back.

I teased her about leaving the next afternoon, she countered with the following week, and by the end of it we'd decided to leave in a few months, at the tail end of winter, because utterly abandoning all your obligations seems more reasonable when you schedule it farther out.

This was going to be the first trip Kati and I took together, though we'd known one another for years. We first met during our freshman year of high school, thrown together by honors classes and extracurricular activities targeting awkward, intelligent girls who had yet to grow into their features. We would share notes and edit one another's English papers, and she would try to dissuade me from having a crush on a guy who would, years later, pick as his social media profile picture an image of him wearing a giant diaper and bonnet while chugging a beer.

The point is, Kati always had better judgment than I.

While my brain has mercifully blocked out most of my memories from the early years of our relationship, one remains clear in my mind and serves as a good microcosm for my and Kati's friendship.

The film *Titanic* came out our senior year of high school, and the student officers decided to make this the theme for our prom. Presumably because they figured the only way to make a room full of dry-humping teenagers in rented tuxedos and ill-fitting Jessica McClintock dresses *more* romantic is pairing it with the tragic, icy deaths of 1,500 people.

The pre-prom assembly involved students acting out selected scenes from the historically dubious film in front of their peers. At one point, a massive paper iceberg crashed into the front of the stage, which had been decorated to look like the ill-fated ocean liner, and a bunch of students spilled out on the floor of the gym, writhing and dying. This understandably took precedence over our classes.

At the dance itself, which was held at the Seattle Aquarium (a small detail that I find both perverse and delightful, considering the circumstances), the backdrop for our formal portraits featured a giant iceberg and the doomed *Titanic* heading straight for it. It was in front of this that we smiled brightly—myself included—with our dates, documenting forever our youthful callousness and the ability of time to not only temper a tragedy but to adapt it into a *great* motif for high school dances.

But Kati's pose for her photo was this: she, making a face of poorly feigned horror, pointing to the iceberg while her friends smiled sweetly and obliviously in front of her. The caption could have read, "Oopsies! They're all going to die!"

When someone is able to rise above the absurdity of teenage life, to point it out for all its ridiculousness, it's best to befriend them immediately. I needed Kati. Even after so many years, this remains true.

* * *

BY JANUARY 2008, IT HAD become clear that my cowork-ers and I weren't going to have jobs for much longer. Weeks went by, projects wrapped up, and no new ones replaced them. Then one morning, we learned that the company was getting bought out by a massive conglomerate on the East Coast. Ownership would officially change hands at the beginning of March, and the very next day they'd scheduled a company-wide meeting. In the intervening weeks, my coworkers and I did what reasonable people do when faced with the inevitable: we took two-hour-long lunches, we polished up our résumés, and we stole whatever wasn't tied down.

There was nothing on the calendar after that meeting—not a single thing for all the days and weeks and months afterward.

And there was nothing to hold me back when Kati said, "Let's do it. Let's go to Italy now."

So, rather than watch the bitter end unfold, I left the coun-try on a chilly February morning, knowing that I would likely not have a job when I returned. My boss Angela wrote me a send-off email that said, simply, "Take care. HAVE FUN FOR ALL OF US."

And though the eight-hour time change between Seattle and Italy proved advantageous (by the time I received the email from my coworker Philip informing me that nearly everyone at the company was out of a job, I'd already had the presence of mind to get drunk), having fun proved elusive. It soon occurred to me that I was losing more than camaraderie and a self-aggrandizing belief that we were making the world a happier place. I was los-ing all the stability and independence that came with a steady income, along with access to that rarely used bathroom on the tenth floor where I could poop in peace. How many places had that?

I had plenty of time to think far too long about all this on the flight over. Unlike normal humans who do not suffer from motion sickness so severe that they get nauseated while checking their watch (please, never ask me the time), I can do very little on flights that won't render me a puking, sweaty heap by the time we land.

Reading a book or familiarizing myself with Vin Diesel's extensive theatrical canon is out of the question. I'm also unable to sleep, which I think is probably a biological safeguard against me asphyxiating on my own vomit at thirty-six thousand feet.

Instead, I sit in my seat for hours, thinking about all the things that happened on the ground that I am presently unable to change. When other people have problems, they meditate, or see a therapist, or try a fad diet in which the only sustenance is words of affirmation from Gwyneth Paltrow. I, instead, save all my introspection and regret for the friendly skies. Mostly this involves me sipping ginger ale while scowling.

Snuggled up close to Kati in the temporal limbo that accompanies international flights, I thought back to when I first started at the game company. Rand and I were living together in a small apartment in North Seattle. He was an entrepreneur, which meant that he'd spent his early twenties wearing hoodies and going into serious debt starting his own company. Unable to find steady work, I had been stringing together as many temp jobs as possible, hoping that if I mashed them together they would sort of resemble a Frankenstein's monster of a career, minus the health insurance.

This job had changed all that. I was able to pay the rent and spend money on frivolities like new shoes and root canals.

When I got home, it would all be over. And so I crisscrossed all over Italy, heavyhearted and trying to enjoy a vacation that was as fiscally reckless as the company's last few months had been.

* * *

I CANNOT DEFINITIVELY SAY WHEN it was that Kati and I first fell ill. A safe estimate puts it at somewhere between five and ten minutes after landing, that upon breathing the sweet citrus-scented Italian air and realizing that the only obligation we had for the next two weeks was to eat copious amounts of carbs and to enjoy ourselves, our immune systems collectively said, "Fuck it."

Whatever the case, it felt instantaneous: upon landing, Kati and I were struck by a virus that, had we been heroines in a Victorian novel, would have killed us. By the time we reached her cousin's home in Genoa several hours later, she was already rationing out the few doses of NyQuil that we found at the bottom of her toiletry bag with a frugality usually found in someone who had been through the Great Depression.

Over the next few days, she and I would take turns sneaking into the bathroom to down water by the cupful so as not to alarm her relatives. When they learned of our illness, they shared with us the rather confounding wisdom that too much water would make us sicker. Kati and I didn't argue, which is the best course of action when dealing with full-blooded, native Italians (never debate people whose ancestors conquered most

of the known world while wearing mini-skirts and sandals). Instead, we simply smiled and excused ourselves to suck on the
bathroom tap while trying not to aspirate a lung.

We'd been staying with Kati's cousin Silvio and his parents in Genoa. After several days of watching Kati and I lying
around, emitting low, miserable moans, Silvio decided that he
needed to show us around, rather than have us squander our
vacation watching *House, MD* dubbed into Italian.

I had mixed feelings about this plan. We were very close
to Cinque Terre, supposedly one of the most beautiful parts of
Italy, and arguably the world, but listen: the dubbed version of
House in Italy is a masterpiece. Since MD doesn't mean anything in Italian, the announcers called the show *House*, MED-
ICAL DIVISION. They practically shouted that last bit, in
heavily accented Italian.

"ME-DEE-CAL DEE-VISION!"

I'm not sure if the soundtrack is actually different, or if it's
simply because they are now speaking the language of Tosca,
but the show feels infinitely more dramatic.

Every few minutes someone would look off camera and ask,
accompanied by a thundering musical crescendo, "Que fac-
ciamo, House?"

And then House would reply, in equally dramatic fashion,
"Non lo so." Cue deafening piano accompaniment.

In the haze of my illness, I was enthralled. Plus, I was learning all sorts of critical Italian vocabulary, like the words for
chlamydia, lupus, and one-night stand. (The last one being a *co-
noscente di una notte*—literally, "an acquaintance of one night."
It's profoundly poetic and nonjudgmental, which makes sense
from a country that reelected Berlusconi.)

Despite my claims that sitting around watching any one of Italy's three television channels while simultaneously eating green pasta was a viable way to appreciate the country and its culture, Kati was hell-bent on actually seeing Italy. Since she was sicker than I was, I relented; when Silvio generously offered to take us to the Cinque Terre on one of his days off, we agreed.

The three of us took the train to Monterosso from Genoa. Slowly, as we rolled south along the coast, the sun began to burn off the marine layer, and I could see the Ligurian Sea, calm and shimmering and blue green. I'd never seen the Italian Riviera.

The Cinque Terre are a cluster of five small towns that sit on the northern Italian coast, built precariously into the cliffside and right up to the water's edge. Our train arrived in the northernmost village of Monterosso. The town is a long crescent that mimics the curve of the turquoise bay it looks out upon. The shoreline is flanked with sun-bleached buildings the same creamy color as the beach. It was too early in the year for sunbathers, who would overrun Monterosso in the coming months, but there were people clustered along the shore, sipping coffees as they enjoyed the view. We walked around, taking in the sunshine, snapping a few photos, and doing what I thought was an admirable job of not collapsing into a feverish heap on the piazza.

The specifics of what happened next will likely remain up for debate in Kati's family for many years. But as she and I remember it, her cousin casually asked us if we wanted to go for a little walk.

That is what we both, specifically, recall him saying. *Una piccola passeggiata.*

In his defense, there is no word in Italian for "hike." Certainly no phrase for a "two-hour-long-journey-that-you-may-not-survive."

You can see why we readily agreed to *una piccola passeggiata*.

In hindsight, I suppose most things that go awry do so incrementally, and I should have realized that. The bowl cut that I somehow elected to have just as I went into the sixth grade (I still do not know how this happened, but my mother, to her credit, did try to stop me) was not a matter of one swift cut but many calculated snips. The demise of the game company where I had been employed had not been the result of any one act. Instead, it was a series of small decisions, each one mostly innocuous on its own, but together resulting in the financial mess that meant the company was selling pennies on the dollar.

And likewise, the "little" hike from Monterosso to Vernazza happened slowly, one feverish step at a time.

It was a long while before Kati and I actually realized what was going on. Silvio was a good stretch ahead of us, and we followed, dutifully, not wanting to seem ungrateful to Kati's cousin, who had selflessly given up his day off to lead us to our deaths on a picturesque mountain.

The sun we'd been basking in back in Monterosso was now beating down upon us. The trail was steep, rocky, and dry. With each step we kicked up a little bit of dust that fell on our newly washed hair and stuck to the backs of our already parched throats. I realized that none of us had thought to bring water. I'd figured that if I needed hydration, I'd just down a couple of frozen confections. But there was nothing—no people, no signs, and certainly no gelato stands—in sight.

It was Kati who finally spoke up.

"Silvio," she said, pausing to wheeze and release a well-timed but nevertheless genuine cough, "how much longer until? . . ."

She let her question trail off there, realizing that she didn't know how to finish. Neither of us knew where we were going.

He looked around noncommittally, as though the landscape—rocky, unwelcoming, and covered in bramble—might provide a reply.

"I'm not sure," he said. "If we pass anyone, I'll ask them."

For another ten treacherous minutes, we encountered no one save for a few feral dogs that lived high up on the mountains. We would eventually come across two hikers who stared at Kati and me with looks usually reserved for three-legged kittens or children who'd cut their own hair.

Silvio chatted with them while Kati and I drifted in and out of consciousness.

"Good news," he said, as the hikers skipped down the hill, flaunting their hydration and appropriate footwear. "It's only another hour or so to Vernazza."

Kati and I let this horrifying information sink in. Somehow, we, feverish and sick, had inadvertently agreed to a nearly two-hour-long dusty hike under the searing Italian sun between two of the five towns of the Cinque Terre.

It was around that time that my dear friend, the voice of reason and moral compass for my teen years, turned to me and whispered, "I'm going to kill him."

"You can't," I replied. "He's the only one who knows where we're going."

I don't remember much of the rest of that trek. It is lost to illness, to the sun, to the dust and heat of that mountainside. I only remember when we rounded a corner, breaking through the prickly, dry shrubs, and saw Vernazza for the first time below us.

Perhaps it was the sacrifice of the time and what was left of our immune systems that made it look as it did. There is a distinct chance that I may have been hallucinating. Or perhaps it really was that beautiful. Whatever the reason, Vernazza was, at that moment, the loveliest place I had ever seen.

From this angle, we could see it perfectly—the buildings were crowded together, a messy pile of jewel-colored little boxes. They extended from near the top of the mountain all the way to the water, carving out a small harbor in the turquoise blue waters of the Ligurian Sea. It had all the unplanned precariousness of a tower built by toddlers: bright, chaotic, and leaving you with the sensation that at any moment, it might go tumbling down.

Even now, when I consider that the hike likely prolonged our illnesses, causing us to be miserably sick for the entire duration of our trip, I have no regrets about not murdering Silvio on that hillside.

This is the strongest testament to the beauty of Vernazza that exists.

When we reached the bottom we found a café where Kati and I, starved and exhausted, ate lunch while Silvio stared at us with a look of terror (and, I would like to think, a measure of admiration) on his face. Have you ever seen how pythons eat? How they swallow adorable woodland creatures whole and without chewing? It was like that but way faster and with bruschetta. When we'd finished, Silvio asked us if we wanted to hike back. Kati emitted a low guttural growl and I pushed her knife out of reach.

We took the train.

In the coming months, I'd think about that hike we took. How I'd never have done it if I'd known what lay ahead of us. I'd have stayed in Monterosso, safe and comfortable. And I'd have missed the sight of Vernazza from above, now indelible in my memory. I'd probably also have gotten better sooner, but that's antithetical to the moral of this story, which is this: sometimes it's best not to know what you are up against; if you are acutely aware of the challenges involved, you'd never do a damn thing. Being clueless is weirdly empowering. You can't worry about the things that you don't yet know you should be worried about. You end up doing wonderful things that you never would have had you been the least bit informed. You run off to Italy. You take horrific and beautiful hikes. You ruin your hair and your makeup and any chance of a future political career. And when it's all over, you can't help but feel anything but incredibly, overwhelmingly grateful.

A week later we'd made our way from Genoa to Naples, and I received the not-at-all surprising news that I no longer had a job. It came over email. A quick note from Philip, from his personal account, because his work account had already been closed. It was over. My layoff wouldn't be official until I got back, so for my remaining week of vacation I was left in a sort of limbo.

I can't remember what I wrote back. I just remember leaning back on the stiff bed of our Naples hotel, Kati hovering over me, her face gently etched with concern.

"You okay?" she asked.

I didn't answer right away. Perspective would eventually come to me. It would hit me after talking to friends who'd also

lost their jobs but had to contend with mortgages and car pay-
ments and feeding their children. I would find it after realizing
that the rest of the world, when faced with setbacks, did not
have the luxury of running off to a foreign country, drowning
their sorrows in massive plates of carbonara and countless cups
of mint chocolate chip gelato. That they did not have dark-eyed
men waiting for them back home, ready to make everything
right.

I would learn that I didn't know a damn thing about hard-
ship. That when someone asks you what you do, there are worse
things in the world than having to answer "nothing" or "I haven't decided yet" or pretending you don't speak English. That
being adrift in a sea of blue enamel paint wasn't that scary when
you had a secure-enough lifeboat.

Lying on that bed in Naples, with Kati staring at me, a mixture of concern and amusement on her face, I didn't know any
of this yet. I didn't know anything, really. In particular, I had no
idea what to do next.

I told her this, and she nodded. She made me drink a glass
of water and then led me out into the dark, winding streets of
Naples in search of gelato.

2

SOMETIMES YOU RUN SCREAMING FROM THE PERSON YOU'RE MADLY IN LOVE WITH

KATI LAID A TRAIL OF biscotti crumbs behind her and I dutifully followed them, eventually making it back to the States. I briefly considered staying in Italy and consuming so much gluten that I'd eventually transform into some sort of human-lasagna hybrid, but several things called me back home, back to Seattle: I couldn't be formally laid off until I showed up at the office in person. My resources (both in terms of clean under-wear and finances) were running low. And most importantly, I missed Rand.

Our wedding date was a few months away, in September. I hadn't planned on throwing the biggest party of my life while newly unemployed. But I'd started to accept that nothing ever goes as planned. The absurd, nausea-inducing-for-onlookers love affair that I found myself in was a testament to that.

When I'd first met Rand six years earlier, at the end of 2001, on the late night bus heading back to Seattle's University District, I was looking for someone who

- was not an alcoholic,
- owned a bed (and not, say, a futon shared with roommates who worked the night shift),
- knew my name (I was flexible on this point, and willing to respond to Gertrude, Genevieve, Jennifer, Giselle, or Gwendolyn. Not Gretchen. Never Gretchen.), and
- wanted to have sex with me.

Please note that love is conspicuously absent from this list.

I was in a funk. My college boyfriend had dumped me unceremoniously the summer before, in the wake of both of my grandparents passing away. ("She handled that well," said absolutely no one.) I'd spend the next few months devising shortsighted ways of easing my loneliness, which usually involved a frat boy and bottom-shelf liquor.

I would eventually seek out a therapist when I realized that my current methods for handling my depression (which can best be summed up as "Eating gyros while crying") were proving ineffective. She dumped me after three sessions.

Had I been an artist, this would have been known as my Blue Period. But since I was twenty-one and a communications major, it is known as my "Midori Sour Period."

I'd even gone so far as to tell my roommate I was through with relationships, which, if sincerely spoken, was a profoundly stupid thing to say. Those words are essentially an incantation to the heavens to send you the love of your life. Precisely when you are most miserable, and angry, and completely fed up with things, and love is more or less the last thing on your mind, that's when it appears, screams something incoherent directly into your face, and crawls down your pants.

It does not care whether you are ready for it. It does not care if your hair looks good. It absolutely does not care if your life is an utter mess.

In November 2001, I, thoroughly intent on being a crazed, sad shut-in for the rest of my days, ran for the bus and crossed paths with the man who would spoil all my plans. In a move ripped from the pages of a terrible romantic comedy, he was standing up to give his seat to—I kid you not—a little old lady.

I should have known then that I was doomed.

We had dinner together a few weeks later, at a candlelit Italian restaurant that was so dangerously romantic I considered faking an illness in order to escape, but the only thing I could come up with was bubonic plague, and the heyday for that is sort of over. Besides, the appetizers had already arrived by then, so I tried to convince myself we'd just be better off as friends.

I'd concluded that was all I had room for in the maelstrom of my life—a friendship with a funny, sweet man whose eyes were the precise shade of brown usually found on frightened baby deer. I looked over at him across the table and silently promised not to kiss him. I kept this resolution for the better part of three hours.

In hindsight, I have to admire my restraint.

✳ ✳ ✳

HERE'S THE THING: I'M NOT a believer in love at first sight. (There are a few caveats. If someone bears a striking resemblance to a *young* Harrison Ford or we're talking about cake, all bets—along with my pants—are off.) I just don't think that you can look at someone you barely know and promise, "I will, during some distant and particularly virulent bout of intestinal discomfort that has afflicted you, clean up the poop splatter that you unknowingly left on the underside of the toilet seat, all while withholding comment." And let's be honest with ourselves: there is no better litmus test for love than dealing with another human being's bodily fluids and not (figuratively) rubbing it in their face afterward.

I'm pretty sure it's in Corinthians.

Love is patient; love is kind. It does not envy; it does not boast; it does not make a big deal about who cleaned up whose shit.

With the exception of the tender sort of madness new parents feel for their children (most of which can be explained away by oxytocin and sleep deprivation), that sort of thing doesn't develop overnight. It grows slowly, so that you don't even realize what it is at first. You just know that at one point in time you were a functional, normal human being with a debilitating fear of coliform bacteria. And some time later you find yourself staring at a toilet brush and realizing that every love song and poem and sonnet that's ever graced your ears suddenly makes sense.

Instead of striking like lightning, it grows slowly, under the most unlikely of circumstances and in the most terrible settings. Under buzzing florescent lights. While you are getting blisters from uncomfortable shoes and the rent is overdue. When someone is serenading you with Bryan Adams's seminal ballad,

"Summer of '69" (a mating ritual that, much to your chagrin, was shockingly effective). That's what's incredible about love. It's nothing like the movies. It happens to mere mortals, manifesting while they're standing in line for groceries or getting a dental check-up or renewing their license at the DMV.

I'm lying about that last one. Love has never, ever thrived at the DMV. That place is where love goes to die. But I'm pretty sure those other examples are sound.

And dear god, it can be utter hell. It took me years to figure things out. First I had to yell, and cry, and break up with him on two occasions (for a total of three hours) before immediately reconciling. I may have, in a petrified move during the early days of our relationship, made out with some random guy with a tongue piercing and several misguided tattoos.

The problem wasn't Rand. The problem was that—and my apologies to Huey Lewis and the News, but it must be said—I'd been completely misled about the power of love.

What we've been lied to about since we were small is that love can fix things when they are broken, instantly. That it can fix us. We are taught to believe that love is a transformative magic wand that turns pumpkins into coaches and dissolves belly fat and makes our teeth whiter. And all of this, supposedly, happens in an instant.

What we aren't told is the truth: that love can actually complicate the fuck out of things. It doesn't take away all the crap that existed before. It just adds a layer to it. If your life was messy before someone loved you, it will still be messy afterward. (It might even be worse, because now you need to wash the sex out of your sheets more often.) We aren't told that it takes years to figure things out, and even then, you still might not.

It's understandable to be petrified by that. To not want to have your understanding of the world completely turned on its head, to not want to have to do more laundry, to not want to navigate a relationship when you literally can't even *pay* a mental health professional to commit to you.

So you start to put unreasonable expectations on that love as a means of getting away from it. You think because someone hasn't instantly fixed your life that they are not the one you should be with. Sometimes, you will put them, and yourself, through hell just to prove that point.

But the real manner in which love works is much subtler. It does fix things. Or maybe, more accurately, it makes *you* fix things. You start to realize that if someone else loves you that much, maybe you should try to love yourself a bit more.

Admittedly, that sounds a little cheesy. And it's in direct opposition to everything we learned from *Beauty and the Beast*, *The Little Mermaid*, and the 1987 Kim Cattrall–Andrew McCarthy tour-de-force, *Mannequin*. Those stories taught us that love is what will save you. Love is literally what will make you human.

But why can't *you* be the one that controls that? What if you start trying to become someone who's worthy of the adoration of this weirdo who keeps telling you that you are wonderful and who won't leave your bed. And after a while, you start thinking maybe they aren't so weird. You learn about their favorite movie and what makes them angry and how their hair looks when they first wake up in the morning. You stop crying. You realize that they don't need to fix the problems in your life, because you can fix it all your damn self.

You still worry about where things are headed, but you keep going anyway. You see where things go.

This was the effect that Rand's affections had on me: slowly, I started to become a better person. I tried to be as good to him as he was to me. I found myself competing with him to see who could be the better partner. (He always won, but I had my moments. Like Valentine's Day 2005, when he came home to me dancing naked to that CD he had wanted. It was the sort of unabashed, absurd display of adoration that can only happen when you are twenty-four, not entirely sure what the hell you are doing, and madly in love.) It was utterly obnoxious to those forced to witness it (the love, I mean. Not the dancing. I'm pretty sure only Rand saw that). My friends said that they were going to be sick, and I graciously handed out vomit bags.

The problem is, most love stories don't focus on slow-simmering, shaky romance that takes its time to come to a rolling boil, even though that's what most of us experience (and that's if we're lucky). It's just not all that interesting. If Jane Austen were alive today, she'd be forced to have Mr. Darcy and Lizzie get together in the first twenty-five pages (also, Darcy would be into sadomasochism).

They would never fight about finances or take things the wrong way or get cold feet.

There is no place for those of us who are afraid or unsure, who wade slowly into the water and occasionally get freaked out by an oncoming wave, running off to make out with pierced strangers whose names we never bothered learning. (Oh, my god. *Wait*. I think it was Nathan. One of them was definitely a Nathan. And maybe there was a Jeff in there, too, somewhere.) But I'd argue that those of us who take our time—who scrutinize and deliberate and wonder if this is the right choice because life is *really* short when you think about it—never question our decisions. When you've already hashed out every neurotic doubt, the only thing left is utter conviction that there is no one else in the world with whom you'd rather spend your days.

I should back up here and tell you why Rand is so wonderful. I've written pages about it already—on my blog, in a tattered journal at the bottom of my bookcase left over from my college years—but the real sign of my love is this: I know every annoying thing about him, and I still adore him. There are no skeletons in the closet. We pulled them all out and put them on the couch, and they are a *great* conversation piece.

I would like to go over some of his more annoying habits now, much as I did in our wedding vows.

- He gets really cranky when he's hungry but refuses to acknowledge that said crankiness is a result of hunger.
- He knows that I like to board a plane as soon as our row is called (ostensibly because I want to have room in the overhead compartment to store my bag, but I think primarily because of hazy childhood memories of being picked last during kickball). Consequently, he waits until just that moment to vanish. After I've dissolved into a panic, he will reappear eating a fro-yo and ask me what is wrong.
- He becomes an insufferable whiner whenever the weather climbs above 75 degrees.
- The night before a trip, after I've spent the week doing all of our laundry, Rand will ask me if I've washed a particular article of clothing. "If it was in the hamper, it's washed!" I will tell him gleefully, still dizzy from Woolite fumes. Inevitably, said article of clothing will not be in

the hamper. It will be hanging in the closet or tucked away in a drawer, completely indistinguishable from the clean clothes therein, and I am *somehow* supposed to know that it's dirty.

• He eats Raisinets, arguably the worst candy ever made.

But here's the thing: I knew this going in. By the time Rand proposed, I was acutely aware of every flaw and shortcoming and knew that I could live with all of them. I knew what delighted him (underbaked cookies, the work of Mel Brooks, the time that I was talking in my sleep and insisted I worked for the Teenage Mutant Ninja Turtles) and what he hated (overcooked pasta, name-dropping, and phone calls that could have easily been handled over email).

I knew he was a generous tipper and an ardent feminist, that he was terrible at putting dirty clothes in the hamper, that he almost always smelled wonderful, but not in an overpowering way. I knew that he loved Marc Chagall and dark chocolate and me.

I knew that I could clean the toilet we shared and not make a big deal about it. I could do that for the rest of my life.

By the time he proposed, I knew exactly what I was getting into.

We were married in Ashland, Oregon. As with my husband, I took my time falling in love with the small town that sits near the Oregon-California border. When I first saw it, I didn't even know where I was. Now I wonder why I spend time anywhere else.

That's the thing about favorite people and favorite places— at one point in your life, they are all uncharted territory. There's no alchemy that transforms them into the loves of your life.

Usually, you just need time to figure it out. They earn your love. And if you are very, very lucky, you might earn theirs.

It was the summer of 2003, a couple of years into our relationship. I'd just graduated from college into the worst job market in decades and Rand, a recent college dropout who was swimming in debt, was about to turn twenty-four, so we decided to celebrate by taking a road trip. We were broke but figured we could break routine and fight in a cramped KIA Spectra, as opposed to our cramped one-bedroom apartment, and the change of pace would be good for us. (The early years of our relationship were tumultuous. He was plagued by creditors, and I was plagued by self-doubt.)

On one scorching July afternoon during that tempestuous trip, Rand and I were driving through the hills of southern Oregon. I can't remember where we were heading or where we'd come from—those details have been sacrificed to time. I only know that we were lost, and when we first saw the little town, nestled in a valley and surrounded by hills turned golden in the dry heat of summer, we breathed a sigh of relief (I'd seen enough horror movie trailers to know that bad things happened to young couples who got lost on road trips).

Rand took a photo of me that day. I am standing by the side of a dusty road, dressed in a skirt and tank top but inexplicably wearing shearling boots. (The early 2000s were a crazy time. Everyone was piercing their eyebrows and tattooing Chinese characters on their bodies. I am grateful I escaped with just one seasonably inappropriate pair of shoes.) The hills loom behind me like waves of burnished brass, and I am smiling at the man behind the camera, entirely unaware that one day he and I would get married here.

But that's how it goes. These things take time. You start weaving a story together and you wake up one day to find that it comprises huge sections of your life. That without that person, something would be missing.

We had lunch outside on a quiet patio, and I forbade Rand from asking the server where we were because it made us look suspicious.

"Only criminals have lunch in random towns that they didn't plan on being in," I explained. He just stared at me quietly for a while. He does that a lot.

The stillness would be broken by a sea of gray-haired retirees that emerged from one of the buildings. Rand and I stared at one another, dumbfounded, trying to figure the reason behind the huge congregation of old people flooding the streets. Was it a meeting of the local chapter of the Werther's Original Fan Club? A Sam Waterston lookalike contest that was admirably gender agnostic? A midterm election? Stumped, we finally asked our server what was going on.

"The plays just got out," she explained.

And then it clicked. In the Pacific Northwest, Ashland is whispered like an incantation among those of us who secretly looked forward to English class in high school, who spent too much time engrossed in sonnets, who were destined to keep our virginities until our twenties because we knew any romance we'd experience would pale next to that of Benedick and Beatrice's (and maybe also because no one would sleep with us). I'd heard of this place plenty of times but had never seen it.

The story is that in the early 1930s, Angus Bowmer, a fellow Washingtonian, University of Washington alum, and quintessential theater nerd, headed down to Ashland to take a job at the nearby university. In 1935, he managed to persuade the town leaders to hold a Shakespeare Festival, complete with an outdoor theater. It would become an annual occurrence, growing into the internationally renowned Oregon Shakespeare Festival.

Bowmer died in 1979. During his time at OSF, he produced Shakespeare's entire canon, directed thirty productions, and performed thirty-two roles. In 1970, the OSF opened up a six-hundred-seat theater named in his honor. When asked if he could have dreamed that his creation would have grown to this size, his reply was brief.

"All my dreams are open-ended."

In the years since Bowmer started the OSF, the company has been written up in countless national newspapers and received glowing praise from *The New York Times* for its commitment to diversity in casting and focus on the works of emerging playwrights, particularly women and people of color. In what may be the most bourgeoisie compliment I have ever given, the performances in Ashland eclipse virtually everything I've seen in New York or London. I realized that the size of a town doesn't matter—it's what takes place there that's important.

When a tiny hamlet in rural Oregon reinvents itself as a tourist destination for thespian enlightenment, when you see Pericles going for an evening run or Ophelia walking down the street looking remarkably lovely and undrowned, anything becomes possible.

On our second trip to Ashland, Rand and I saw our first play at the OSF, a production of *As You Like It*. On our third visit, after too much wine and not enough crème brûlée, we decided this was where we wanted to get married. On our fourth visit, not long after I returned from my trip to Italy with Kati, we did.

* * *

ON OUR WEDDING DAY, OUR rental car's thermostat read 104 degrees. My dress was crinkled taffeta, and Rand wore a tuxedo with a tag inside that read "Made Expressly for Geraldine's Husband." My family complained about the remote location of our wedding and the heat, and we nodded sympathetically and directed them to the open bar.

They didn't understand why we'd decided to get married down there, and we didn't need them to. That's the great thing about being in love. You don't need to justify it or explain it to anyone. You just need to enjoy it and occasionally be reminded to put on pants.

At the reception, my brother Edward raised his glass and gave one of the best wedding speeches ever composed. I had given him a list of topics that were off-limits. He began by reading it aloud, because that is what my brother does. He says precisely what you don't want him to, and every word of it will be painful and brilliant.

He concluded with this:

"Rand," he said, looking at his new brother-in-law, "you're family now. And that means nobody hurts you . . . but us."

My family, having completely forgotten about the heat and their own discomfort thanks to the amnesiac properties of a chilled rosé, cheered so loudly our champagne glasses rattled, while my new in-laws smiled nervously and clutched their purses.

There, in the middle of those same hills I saw on our first visit, as the sun set and we stood in a field of gold, Rand told me he loved me. As a reply, I pretended to throw up a bit. I also noted that I had taken off my underwear two hours prior because it was too hot and expressed excitement that no one would be able to tell. He just laughed. Like me, he knew exactly whom he was marrying, exactly what he was getting into.

We've returned to Ashland every year for our anniversary. On our fifth visit, I realized that if the air is just right, the entire town smells like lavender. On our ninth visit, my husband revealed that he could touch his tongue to his nose, information which, as his wife, I feel I should have been privy to much, much sooner. On our tenth visit, we found that smoke from wildfires nearby makes the moon look red.

At some point therein, after having visited every continent that isn't primarily inhabited by penguins, I realized that this was my favorite place in the world. It didn't hit me the first time I saw Ashland. Or the second. It happened slowly, until one day I found myself staring at the last traces of sunlight on the surrounding hills and realized there was literally no place else I'd rather be.

Funny how people and places can creep up on you like that, until suddenly you can't live without them.

This is not to say that Ashland is perfect. If love comes from knowing something really, really well, then it comes from knowing all its shortcomings, too.

Here is a brief list of Ashland's:

- It has only one doughnut shop, which is only open until 2:30 p.m. on most days and is closed all day Sunday, which I'm sure you'll agree is total bullshit.
- I once saw a guy let his dog drink directly from a public water fountain.

- The place is overrun with deer and septuagenarians. It's like *Cocoon* meets *Bambi*, which sounds innocuous but in reality is rather terrifying. Also, a lot of them get really angry when you update Shakespeare even the *teeniest* bit. (The old people, I mean. I have no idea how the deer feel about it.)
- Based on a random sampling, at least half of the hotel proprietors in town are assholes.

But here's the thing: none of that really matters to me. After enough visits, I've come to know Ashland's faults and virtues as well as I know my own husband's, and I know I can live with almost all of them. I see them both for what they really are—imperfect, beautiful, and mine.

It didn't happen overnight. It happened slowly, after numerous visits and the creation of countless memories, mostly good and sometimes bad. Some people understand my affinity for it; others don't. I figure that's okay—if Rand is the only person on the planet who understands why I feel the way I feel, that's enough. You love what you love, and you take the good with the bad.

It is simply my favorite place in the world. And as with him, when I finally realized it, I didn't have a single doubt.

3

THE CONTENTS OF MY MOTHER'S CARRY-ON LOOK LIKE EVIDENCE FROM A PRISON RIOT

I'VE HEARD IT SAID THAT we do not simply marry our spouses—we marry their families, too. I often bring this up to Rand, just so it is abundantly clear that he willfully walked into all this. But with the exception of the pickax, now part of family lore, he never seems to mind all that much. He is often kinder and more patient and simply better to my family than I am. I maintain that it's because none of them have ever given him a mullet.

He puts up with my older brothers, my curmudgeonly father, my doting aunts, and my unfiltered uncles. He puts up with a cadre of swarthy cousins and their adorable, sticky progeny (the latter's collective favorite pastime—jamming their

fingers into the mucus membranes of Rand's face). He puts up
with that drunk guy who keeps showing up at family events un-
invited. He puts up with me.

But most significantly, he puts up with my mother. This is
no small feat. She is a destroyer of worlds and logic and the occasional plate.

I have a distinct memory of her chaperoning a field trip
when I was five or six. I really needed to pee and virulently refused to follow her into a bathroom because I thought it was a
broom closet. *Because my mother suggesting I pee in a closet was
not outside the realm of possibility.* I was shocked when there was
actually a toilet for me to use. When I was ten, she led a protest
at Universal Studios because too many of the rides were broken, and secured a refund on admission for us and two dozen
other people (after which we were immediately escorted out of
the park). She yelled at the first boy who ever broke my heart
and at my driver's ed instructor when he made me cry. She broke
up fights. She started wars. She inadvertently taught me way too
many Italian cuss words, an accusation she vehemently denies.

She breaks every rule and she bucks every damn trend, except those that include leopard print. I can't even do a decent
imitation of her accent, despite having heard it nearly every day,
either in person, on the phone, or in my echoic memory for the
last three decades or so—reminding me to triple-check that my
front door is locked so I won't be kidnapped.

Her pattern of speech is an archaeological blueprint—
decipher it, and you can loosely trace the path of her life. A hybrid of an Italian accent (where she was born) mixed with an
English one (where she spent many formative years), softened by
several decades in the United States (which has given it—and

this is truly baffling—a sort of Valley Girl lilt). The best approx-
imation I can come up with is Alicia Silverstone from *Clueless*, if
the film had been set in a Turkish prison.

She sounds rather elegant and charming provided you don't
pay too much attention to what she's actually saying, which usually has to do with aliens or governmental cover-ups about the
existence of said aliens, punctuated every now and then with a
toss of her hair and a flippant "Well, you know, what-*ever.*"

She raised me and my brother Edward bilingually—we
grew up speaking Italian at home and with my grandparents.
It became the language of curses and secrets and scolding—
anything we didn't want someone to overhear was discussed in
Italian.

And yet, despite being able to communicate with my
mother in two languages, I rarely know what she's talking about
and consistently have trouble understanding the logic—such as
it is—behind her actions. It is easier to predict the flight path of
a moth than to know what my mom is going to do next. She is
Loki; she is Eris; she is the avatar for the god of lost socks and
the personification of that feeling you get when you are about to
pay for groceries and realize you don't have your wallet.

I rebelled in the only way I saw fit: I was, despite a predis-
position to swearing like a (bilingual!) sailor in my preschool
years, a good, reliable kid. It wasn't that my mother's way wasn't
appealing—fun and carefree and excitingly dramatic, it was
sometimes too much so. Like having a beautiful wild mare ma-
jestically destroy your bathroom.

I soon recognized my own capacity for chaos, and one of
the few things that kept it in check was that the role had already
been taken.

The position of Beautiful Chaotic Disaster Vixen has been filled. May we recommend something else? Like Responsible Fed-Up Daughter?

I did my homework and occasionally the homework of my friends. I obeyed rules to a fault. I never questioned authority. Even to this day, I plan and organize and make elaborate emergency protocols. Living in the Pacific Northwest, my earthquake survival kit is incredibly well-appointed, except for when I get stoned and eat all the rations. But I almost always immediately replace them.

I spent long hours scrutinizing her behaviors like a biologist studying another species. I know that this isn't unique to us. Most people I know are bewildered by their parents, and I suspect that's the whole point. They raise us, they feed us, and they do illogical and strange things that confuse us, so that when we go out into the world and encounter illogical and strange things, we aren't scared. If anything, we feel right at home.

This is how I've come to explain her behavior—as simply preparing me for whatever life threw at me. Absent of this justification, most of her actions become just inscrutable. Or felonious. Or both. I'd like to say that I patently disagree with everything she's ever done, but then she goes and yells at Rick Steves *in person* for what she perceives as an unfair bias against southern Italy, and I find myself snickering with delight. I've spent years trying to anticipate her actions so I could somehow be ready for them. So I'd be ready for anything.

It was fruitless, but know that I tried. I really did.

I tried to warn Rand. During the first year of our relationship, we took our first cross-country trip together. In the weeks before, I had attempted to explain what traveling with my mom was like—that her mere presence on a trip made the Punic Wars seem like not that big a deal. We were headed down to Florida with my mother to visit family for Christmas. My motivations were simple: I was going to arguably the worst state in the union during the holiday season because of love and also guilt. Rand, I can only assume, was going out some sort of Victorian self-flagellation.

Rand booked the tickets for us; we got Mom an aisle seat, which she prefers. I casually suggested that we also book her on a different departing flight. I may have added a little laugh at the end of it, which he mistook for me joking, and not a failed suppression of my own hysteria.

Don't get me wrong: my mother is a lovely person, and in many ways, she's remarkably unfussy and easy to please, especially when it comes to travel. She's willing to sleep on the floor and she'll eat anything, be it decorative soaps ("I thought they were chocolate") or canned meat. But she is not predictable. She is as subtle and unobtrusive and law-abiding as her homeland, which is to say, not at all.

She once packed for my cousin's wedding by doing an entire load of laundry and dumping all of it into her bag. It consisted mostly of lingerie. Whereas I once had a meltdown of unreasonable proportions when I left for a trip and realized I'd forgotten my usual dental floss and had to rely on the backup floss I keep in my purse.

Mom tries to leave the house in a negligee, so I carry *backup floss*. (Rally the psych majors! I am the case study they *dream* of.)

Her influence on my life has been that of an exquisite tornado: she tears through a room noisily, a whirlwind of anxious affection, leaving a path of destruction and lipstick marks in her wake. She creates chaos out of order, but she can also do the opposite: place her in the middle of a disaster and she will calmly set things right. She can't come over to dinner without bringing two pounds of food with her and insisting on doing all the dishes afterward, breaking only one or two glasses in the process.

She's fun. And interesting. She'd make a great travel partner were it not for the fact that you'd never reach your destination, because she's gotten you locked up in some prison where you get a body cavity search in lieu of due process.

I tried to express this to Rand, and he gently dismissed my worries.

He found my mother entertaining and mostly harmless. He'd met Melba, the mannequin she kept in her home. The first time Rand was over at my mom's house, she insisted on introducing him to the life-size plaster figure, a relic from some 1950s department store, missing two hands. My mother proceeded to have an animated, one-sided conversation with Melba while my future husband nodded mutely. This was three short weeks into our relationship; he could have run. He had his chance.

In hindsight, we should have paid attention to the fact that the person who had known my mother for more than two decades and had emerged from her womb was in a panic, and the guy who had known her for less than a year was not.

"It will be fine," he said. "You just need to relax."

I did precisely the opposite, but more quietly than I had been, which I felt was a good compromise. By the time we reached the airport on the day of our departure, I was by all outward appearances fine, save for a twitch underneath my left eye that began firing then and has continued ever since.

If you have managed to avoid the airport during the holidays, congratulations. I would love to meet in order to learn your secrets and also to slap you, Joan Collins–style, out of jealousy. The rest of us know well that had Dante ever flown cross-country in late December, *The Inferno* would have had a tenth circle of hell.

It was a week or so before Christmas and fifteen months after 9/11. The United Airlines check-in desk had been taken over by feral children. At the other kiosks, agents were working tirelessly to send checked baggage to destinations they picked at random. Everyone in line at JetBlue was openly weeping.

And we were about to go through a heightened security screening with my mother.

"Mom," I said, as we approached the checkpoint, "no jokes."

"Hmm? . . ."

"No jokes, okay? Don't say anything inappropriate."

"Of course not."

"I'm serious. No cracks about"—here I lowered my voice—"terrorism or plane crashes or anything like that."

My mom nodded, but I pressed on for the next few minutes, outlining in a hushed whisper all the potentially disastrous things I didn't want her to say.

"You know," she finally said, turning to look at me, "this is really offensive. I'm not stupid."

This is a skill of my mother's—to act reasonable for just long enough to make you second-guess yourself. Despite having more than twenty years of experience on my side, I quickly backpedaled and apologized.

This was, after all, a woman who had immigrated to America *while I was in utero* and my brother was three. Just a few years earlier, she'd married my father and moved to Germany without speaking the language, traveling alone to Italy and back by train, with my brother, then a baby, asleep in her arms. By the time I knew her, she spoke three languages and had lived in four radically different countries.

She was even visible in my first passport photo: she's holding a six-month-old me high over her head, her hands visible on either side of me. I am slumping in them like a lump of uncooked dough, squishy and hairless. I can't imagine how this was an acceptable image for an official federal document, but I suspect that was just how things went in the hedonistic world of the 1980s. People were doing lots of cocaine and wearing shoulder pads, and even the Ghostbusters were smoking. In light of this, having someone else's hands in your passport photo seems perfectly reasonable.

Despite her quirks and erratic behavior, she clearly knew how to travel and through it had acquired a unique kind of badassery found almost exclusively in immigrants. The sort of toughness that comes from jumping headfirst into a foreign country and a foreign culture and a foreign language and saying, "I got this."

I had to start giving her more credit, I resolved. Especially when it came to travel.

I was about thirty seconds into my resolution, waiting in line for the metal detector, when I heard her yelling behind me.

"HELP ME."

I turned around. My mother was crouched on the ground, frantically clawing at her neck.

"What are you doing?"

"I HAVE TO TAKE OFF MY JEWELRY."

"Why didn't you do that before?"

"JUST HELP ME."

Here is a fascinating fact about my mother: for security purposes, she feels that leaving her valuables at home is unsafe. And so on any given trip she'll wear roughly three dozen individual pieces of jewelry. This one was no different. She looked like a walking homage to Liberace and cubic zirconia.

"Christ, mom, why are you wearing so many necklaces?"

"JUST HELP ME."

She flipped her mass of hair forward, and I looked at the back of her neck. It was a tangle of a half dozen chains of varying sizes, woven through with long strands of her hair. I began fumbling at the many clasps (all impossibly tiny, and some were attached to the ends of other necklaces, just to make things interesting).

The task was made slightly more difficult by the fact that my mother was frantically squirming as she pried her rings off, while a massive rush of holiday travelers tried to get past us. I had most definitely lost sight of my carry-on, which I was fairly certain had been carted away and detonated in the name of national security.

As I took inventory of the contents of my lost bag, I slowly unraveled my mother from her cocoon of jewelry. When she was finally free from her chains, she bounded off for parts unknown like a bunny released from a trap.

I took a deep breath, removed my necklace and watch, and placed my bag on the conveyor belt. The TSA agent opposite me, in his forties and gray-templed, was looking intently over my shoulder.

"Is . . . is that your momma?" he asked in a faint drawl, still staring past me.

I turned around. Mom had set off a metal detector and was now giggling through a pat-down.

"Yes," I said, with a heavy sign of resignation. "That would be she."

"You . . . you tell your momma she's got it *going on.*"

Now, I realize how improbable all this sounds, because I've neglected to provide you with one key piece of information: my mother is, was, and (if trends continue) will likely always be a bit of a knockout.

I can say this without any risk of vanity: we look nothing alike. I got my father's Eastern European features: a nose large enough to require that I have sense of humor, a perpetually pissed-off expression, and a slight but proud mustache.

I am shaped like a sturdy, asymmetrical potato. Built to endure a harsh winter, appealing to anyone who has survived famine.

But Mom looks remarkably like Monica Vitti, an Italian actress who, based on my limited research, spent the better part of the 1960s looking sultry and sad across Italy while eating gelato. Big eyes, full lips, killer cheekbones. Naturally thin with those weird, long muscles that I have spent countless fruitless hours in Pilates class trying to get. And pretty much all of it is fucking recessive.

I remember a dozen or so moments in my childhood when some poor, hapless admirer would try the cringe-worthy tactic of asking me what my mother's name was as I stood there, holding her hand.

"Mom," I usually replied, exasperated the way only children can be—when you've been on the planet for only a few years and someone is wasting a serious percentage of your life. "Her name is Mom."

The point is: this agent's reaction wasn't all that new or surprising.

Rand and I passed through the metal detector, and I stood, waiting for my mother.

Another agent, blond, handsome, thirtyish, pointed to my mother's purse.

"Ma'am, is this yours?"

"It's my mom's," I said, pointing to her on the other side of security.

"I'm just going to run it through again."

I nodded, strangely unconcerned. I'd already spent all my energy taking off her jewelry. I slipped my watch back on and retrieved my bag. Near me, Rand was shrugging on his suit jacket and smoothing out invisible wrinkles.

Mom finally made it through security and walked up to me, barefoot and shockingly small without her usual platform heels.

"That agent is rescanning your bag," I said, gesturing to the front of the x-ray machine. "And that gentleman," I pointed to the salt-and-pepper-haired agent from before, "would like me to inform you that you, quote, 'have got it going on.'"

She giggled.

Mom's bag came through again, and the younger agent explained that he would need to look through it first.

"I just need to check something," he said apologetically. "But it can't be what I thought it was."

Looking back, I consider it a shocking display of filial love that I didn't instantly disavow any knowledge of my mother right then and there. ("I've never met this woman before," I'd say, and walk swiftly to my flight. End of story.) What I'd learned over the years, but what this poor hapless fool did not yet know, was that with my mother, it absolutely *could* be what he thought it was. There were no limits to what her purse could be hiding.

It's kind of like Mary Poppins's bag, if Mary was a compulsive hoarder who hung out with hobos. My mother's purses defy the laws of logic and space-time. When I was a kid, this was delightful, because I could always find some fun treat inside like a fortune cookie or a book of matches or a kitten.

But as an adult I've learned to fear the contents of her bag, a reaction that, I realize, can be traced back to precisely this moment.

The security agent rummaged through my mom's carry-on. It was strangely shaped—deep, but rather narrow, so he couldn't actually open it enough to see what he was doing. He was just reaching in blindly and pulling things out by touch, as if it were some sort of terrifying grab bag.

I remember the look on his face when he first felt the chain. His brow furrowed, and his face registered that familiar "I am not paid enough for this" expression worn by so many who worked for Homeland Security.

Slowly, he began to pull the offending object out. Like a magician unfurling a rope of handkerchiefs from his sleeve, or *The Lord of The Rings* trilogy, I expected it to end long before it did. It was a metal chain, roughly three feet long and an inch thick, looped in an enormous ring. My mother's keys came out last, dangling from the end.

"Those are my keys," Mom said, helpfully.

I decided my only recourse was to pretend this behavior was entirely normal and not a deleted scene from *Mad Max*.

"Oh," I said, with a frantic chuckle. "It's just her keys."

The agent shook his head.

"No," he said, "That wasn't what I saw on the scan." My stomach dropped.

He continued rifling through mom's bag. Over her head, Rand caught my eye. He'd been ready to go for some time now—a delay like this was new to him, and I suspect he was starting to understand why I'd insisted we arrive at the airport three hours early and also why we should have left my mother at home.

See? I'm not irrational. I've been worried for A PERFECTLY GOOD REASON.

And that perfectly good reason was what the agent finally pulled out next from my mother's bag.

In my memory, the entire security checkpoint fell silent at that moment. A teacup shattered on the floor. Someone screamed and fainted.

The TSA agent held in his hand a ten-inch-long stainless steel pickax, found in the bowels of my mother's purse.

I was about to say something, but I lost my train of thought as soon as the agent began pulling out retractable blades from the handle. A screwdriver. A corkscrew. A pair of six-inch long blades, one serrated, one not, in the event that you need to stab someone and also slice a baguette.

By now, my mother's packing habits had garnered a small crowd. A cluster of agents had come over to see what was happening. One of them realized the implications of the situation, and what it meant for national security.

"We need to strip search them," he said to the blond agent, eyeing the three of us.

"*All* of them."

Rand blanched. In the distance, Christmas music played. I closed my eyes and wondered what death is like.

But, as has so often been the case, my mother's eccentricities and legally questionable behaviors were ignored on account of how she looked in skintight jeans. Her admirer, the gray-haired agent from earlier, came over, confidently.

"It's okay," he said. "They're fine."

And then, alarmingly: "I know them."

I have told this story many times, and friends have often argued its accuracy. "Why," they inquire, "would someone who found her attractive *not* want her to be strip searched?"

And the answer is, clearly, that this gentleman was playing the long game. He knew that if he saved us from a strip search, his odds of incurring my mother's favor were much higher.

I suppose, in the interest of homeland security, I should have pointed out that we didn't know him. But I didn't want to start our Christmas vacation with a cavity search, so I remained quiet while the agents at the other end of the table discussed our fate. Today, had the same thing happened, we'd be carted off to some island where the only rule is "No one escapes alive." But this was 2002. Not all the protocols were in place. The TSA was not the widespread bastion of mediocrity we've come to know and hate.

The final judgment was merciful: we could get on our flight, dignity/modesty more or less intact. We just had to leave behind mom's pickax. Astonishingly, they let her keep the three-foot length of chain.

I was effusively, absurdly grateful. I was also ready to leave my mother behind, too, if need be.

"But I need that," Mom said, when she realized she might be separated from her pickax.

"Mom, we're leaving it here."

"I need it," she said again, more quietly and somewhat pitifully.

"You can't take it past security," I snapped.

"You could always mail it to yourself," one of the agents suggested.

"Yes. Let's do that," Mom said.

"You'll have to go back to the other side of security," the agent explained. "There's a shipping office—"

"Mom, we are NOT taking it—"

"I NEED IT."

"No, you don't."

"I'll do it," Rand said.

"You'll *what*?"

"I'll do it."

In the coming years, Rand and I would discuss this repeatedly. How it was ridiculous of him. Indulgent, unnecessary. How if the only punishment my mother received for bringing a miniature pickax on a domestic flight in a post 9/11 world was to lose said pickax, she'd have gotten off easily.

Rand has said, time and again, if these events had happened later in our relationship, later in his relationship with my mom, he'd have calmly deposited the pickax in the trash, promised to buy her another one, and boarded the flight while resolutely ignoring her protests. But we'd been dating for barely a year, and we were still doing things that we've since abandoned. I was shaving my legs. He was humoring my mother.

I pleaded with him not to go, panicked that he'd miss our flight. One of the agents said that they'd let him skip the line. Rand told us he'd meet us on board, gave me a quick peck on the cheek, and disappeared, the flaps of his jacket taking flight as he ran into the sea of holiday travelers.

Watching him go, I remember thinking that this act—selfless, idiotic, illogical—was what love was.

In the years since, it hasn't seemed to have waned at all, though he now has fewer qualms about gently telling my mother that she's being fucking insane.

By the time we reached the gate, the plane was well into the boarding process. Mom didn't understand why I wasn't responding to any of her attempts at conversation or how I'd managed to sweat through both my shirts.

"You almost got us strip searched," I finally said, barely above a whisper.

"I got us out of trouble," she countered.

"YOU WERE THE ONE WHO GOT US INTO TROUBLE IN THE FIRST PLACE."

Mom rolled her eyes at me. "Well, what*ever*," she said.

We boarded. Rand had booked himself and me the aisle and middle seat in one row and given Mom the aisle opposite.

"I'm not sitting with you?"

"You like the aisle," I said.

She looked hurt.

"You *like* the aisle," I repeated. "I figured this way we could both have the aisle and still be close to one another."

In what I have to consider a rather marked accomplishment, Mom succeeded in taking offense to this, seeing it as a punishment for what had happened before. As though I could have anticipated the present fiasco and planned our seating arrangements accordingly. Which is ridiculous, because if I had known she was going to get us nearly strip searched, I wouldn't have put her in a different row. I would have put her on a different flight. To a different final destination.

"You like the aisle," I hissed once more. I don't know if she heard me; she was already engrossed with the in-flight magazine and eating almonds, to which she is allergic.

I sat, nervously waiting for Rand. He was the last person to board our plane. He rushed in, his face pink, his forehead damp with sweat.

He passed my mother without acknowledging her and moved into the middle seat next to me.

"Did you want the aisle?"

"No."

"Are you okay?"

He waited a beat before answering.

"They almost didn't let me back through," he said, his voice soft and devoid of emotion. He'd found the shipping office easily but had gotten caught up in security gridlock when he'd tried to make it back through. The agent who had told him that he could skip the line had disappeared. He eventually made it through when someone else recognized him from earlier.

He didn't look at me as he explained what had happened. He only stared ahead at the seat in front of him. His first flight with my mother, and she'd already succeeded in breaking him. We hadn't even begun taxiing.

"I get it," he said, finally turning to me, his eyes wide and glassy. "I get it now."

He didn't elaborate further. There was no need. He understood my anxiety, my fears, the specific sort of madness that overtakes your life when you invite my mother into it. That I was who I was—organized and cautious and overly apologetic—because my mother wasn't.

In the decade and a half since that day, he has come to understand the important role she plays in our lives. That my mother is a prerequisite catastrophe, needed so that we can have order. Not long ago, she and I had a monumental, earth-shaking fight. When I told Rand about it, he shook his head.

"You have to call her. We *need* your mom."

There are a finite number of things we can control and an infinite number of things that we cannot. I've spent my life trying to prepare for every variable, but nothing ever goes as planned, anyway. I suspect that's what my mother realized a long time ago: that there is no point to seeking order. That even when you think everything is in place, the unpredictable is there. It sneaks into your suitcase, in the form of a forgotten nail file or water bottle or the occasional stainless steel pickax with retractable blades. It walks onto a midnight bus and blindsides you with the sort of romance you didn't think actually existed. It hovers on the edge of your passport photo, and you think it doesn't belong there because you've failed to realize that it is holding you up.

Sometimes, you have to stop fighting the chaos and just embrace it.

I looked over at my mother, tiny in her aisle seat, flipping through a magazine, brushing a long strand of wavy hair over her ear. The flight was packed, but the universe had seen fit to reward my mother's behavior. The two seats next to her were vacant. Whoever had booked them had missed their flight.

We flew to Florida, and my mother happily curled up and fell asleep across all three seats.

4

IN WHICH I AM SURPRISED TO LEARN THAT GETTING LOST DOESN'T BRING ABOUT THE APOCALYPSE

IT WAS RAND WHO SUGGESTED I start a blog—just one more way in which he'd decided to ruin all my plans. It was early 2009; it had been a year since my layoff, and during that time I found I was particularly ill-suited to most professions. I'd sent out a bevy of résumés and cover letters, including one that began with the sentence "I believe my diverse skills would make me an excellent water sewer analyst." I had received no replies. I took a few freelance gigs when they appeared, but the bulk of my day was spent in a funk, trying to decide whether I'd let my brain atrophy naturally or expedite the process through recreational drugs.

Rand was concerned that the vast amounts of free time were making me unhinged. It was after a long day that I'd spent perusing Craigslist's "free stuff" section and penning an alarmingly long complaint letter to the manager of the Little Caesar's in Marysville, Washington, about the decline in the quality of their Pizza-Pizza, that he suggested I write for the unnamed masses of the Internet.

"What about?" I asked.

"What do you want to write about?"

"You and cake." I should have pretended to think about my answer more, because Rand let out a defeated sigh and shook his head. He tried a slightly different approach.

"What can you write about every day?"

This time I stopped, considered the question carefully, and answered more slowly.

"You," I said, as though the idea had just come to me. I paused for a long minute, squinting as I stared into nothing.

" . . . and cake."

He closed his eyes and took a deep breath, which is what he sometimes does when he's overcome by his love for me.

"No one will want to read that," he said. And then he offered up the idea of travel. For the last few years, his work had required him to be on the road. And because he was constantly working, he was constantly zipping off somewhere. A travel blog meant that I could write *and* spend time with him. Which sounds like a great idea, but just you wait.

By now, I really should have stopped listening to Rand. Because here's the thing that he won't tell you and he will probably get mad at me for revealing, but I feel you should nevertheless know: Rand has terrible ideas.

If you met him, you wouldn't realize this. He comes across as exceedingly smart and logical, which is precisely what makes him dangerous. He gets these bat-shit crazy ideas, and he looks so nice and normal that they seem totally reasonable. I've seen him order a cappuccino for an eight-year-old. He refuses to get insurance on rental cars because he's "done the math" and it's more financially viable to pay for an accident every few years. One time he put hand soap in the dishwasher, which is fine if you want to do a bunch of ecstasy and turn your kitchen into a 1990s-era bubble bath–themed rave, but not if you want to actually wash dishes. Also, he thinks Oswald acted alone.

He makes the unreasonable sound sane with such regularity that when he suggested I become a travel writer, it seemed like a good idea.

There were, of course, several problems with Rand's idea. The first, and perhaps most salient, was this: I have zero sense of direction.

I know that a lot of people think that about themselves, but I assure you: I am worse. This, and not the big eyes or the pouty lips or the metabolism of a fucking hummingbird, is what I inherited from my mother. I never know where the hell I am, and of course Rand always does. He's able to pick out cardinal directions when we're standing in a city we've never been to. On the rare occasion that he happens to get disoriented, though, he will ask me which direction I think we should head. And then he'll proceed to go the exact opposite way.

Without fail, that will be correct.

Logic would dictate that since I am so consistently wrong, I simply need to always go the opposite of what I think is the right way. Then I'll surely end up in the correct place, right?

But no. That's never the case. My brain is so traitorous that even when I do the opposite of what I think is right, I *still* end up in the wrong place. It's some epic, inevitable-as-a-Greek-prophecy type bullshit where I'm always wrong. Before the blog, my solution to this problem was simple: I never went anywhere alone. As a child, I went so far as to try to convince people to accompany me to the bathroom, even in the comfort of my own home. Success in this endeavor was mixed.

There was other evidence that perhaps I was not cut out for a life on the road, or a life that required any degree of movement at all. I constantly suffer from motion sickness. I feel nauseated after bending over to *tie my shoes*. I'm pretty sure this is the universe's way of saying, "Stay still," and also, "Maybe you shouldn't have survived infancy."

Would that these were the only things that make me a terrible traveler, but the list goes on. I can barely point out Asia on a map. It takes me three hours to pack for anything. I have *dietary restrictions*. I can't sleep on planes. Nor can I watch movies, because staring too intently at a screen makes me feel nauseated. I can't really do anything on a plane without barfing, and that includes barfing. Once I get started, it's basically an infinite loop of puking.

Also, I'm terrified of pigeons.

The point is: I should not be traveling at all (and perhaps shouldn't be let outside my house), much less writing a blog about it. But somehow when Rand suggested it, it sounded perfectly reasonable.

So in the spring of 2009, I started a travel blog. Sometimes you can't let a complete dearth of natural talent or ability stop you from doing something. Imagine where we would be as a society without open-mic night or amateur pornography or those painful preliminary rounds of *American Idol*. I, too, shudder at the thought.

In the early days of my blog, I pretended that I knew what I was doing. I tried to write articles that sounded professional and came up with all sorts of lists that I thought people would find helpful. I had advice about which lip balms to use during long, dry flights and proper footwear suggestions, and I'd even compiled a list of tips on how not to get your luggage stolen (I was particularly ill-suited for this task, as I'd just recently gotten my luggage stolen). It was all incredibly useful and so dull it would have bored someone who was already unconscious.

The worst part, though, was that I started to believe I *knew* what I was doing. I would stride confidently out of my hotel room, and it would be several long blocks before I realized that I didn't know where I was going. Also, I'd already forgotten the name of my hotel. Terrified, I'd usually run back the way I'd come and wait until Rand was free so we could hang out together.

This sort of terrified codependency is not ideal when one is trying to become a travel writer. And it would soon change—thanks to my husband and his illogical career advice.

In the fall of 2009, we'd been married for a year, and I'd been writing the blog for six months. That October, we went back to New York. I like the city. It's full of impatient people and wonderful food and when I'm there, I feel like my finger is on the pulse of everything. Also, I once saw a well-dressed and utterly unassuming young man in Chelsea squat down on the sidewalk, poop, and then pull up his pants and continue walking. I have always found this inexplicably comforting. New

York has the capacity to make you feel incredibly normal and well-adjusted.

As comfortable as I was in the city, I still relied heavily on Rand to figure out where the hell I was going, but I suppose that's true of everything and not simply travel.

It was our last morning in town—Rand had spent the last few days engrossed with his conference, and I swore that I'd go out and explore Manhattan on my own, but I inevitably ended up cloistered in our hotel room, looking up nearby bakeries.

I was terrified of losing my way. Of the vulnerability that accompanies stepping off a subway or out of a cab and realizing you have utterly no idea where you are. My mother, despite all her charming recklessness, imbued in me a deep, debilitating fear of everything. I try not to judge her too harshly for this act. She was new to America, and I was the first girl born in my generation of the family, after seven boys. Apparently everyone got together, saw my tiny vagina, and collectively freaked the fuck out. They decided that the only way to keep it (and me) safe was to make sure I firmly believed that the world was out to kill me. I try to be forgiving of the sheer terror they instilled in me. They simply wanted me to live a long, safe, petrified life.

The problem was, their tactic worked far too well. If anxiety were a component of a long life (it is not), I and my neuroses would never die. The thing I would later learn is that the world isn't dangerous. I mean, parts of it are, but unless you step directly into a volcano or cover yourself in raw meat and traipse across the Serengeti, you should be okay. Some people are dangerous, sure, but they are few and far between and often not found in modern-day Midtown Manhattan. If you let your fear of them control your life, you are utterly fucked.

But I hadn't realized that yet and was still scared of everything surrounding me. My coping mechanism was to try to control every single variable that I could. And to never, ever, get lost. It didn't matter that I could ask any number of passersby for help, or that my deepest fear—that I would somehow become so utterly disoriented that I'd never see the people I loved ever again—made zero sense. Fear doesn't need logic to thrive. Often it does perfectly well without a hint of it. Some of the most illogical people I know are perpetually terrified.

So I became intimately acquainted with the interior of the Midtown Sheraton, venturing out only when my reserves of cupcakes were running low or I just desperately needed a whiff of the mixture of stale urine and grilled meat and car exhaust that imbues every inch of Manhattan, with the exception of the Meatpacking District (which mostly just smells like sex—and also grilled meat). I'd reduced the greatest city in the world to a comfortable radius of a few square blocks.

But on that last day we'd already checked out of our hotel room and Rand had work obligations, so I found myself marooned on a couch in the lobby, alone and somewhat panicked. I'd already exploited all of Midtown: I'd spent hours at MoMA; I'd walked up and down Fifth Avenue; I'd visited the guy selling candied peanuts so many times that I was beginning to dream up disguises I'd use the next time. Because this was in the dark years before smart phones, and I was without a laptop or an Internet connection, I had no idea what to do next. The only thing in my possession was a small laminated map I'd picked up at the museum.

I unfolded it, staring at the grid of streets, hoping they'd make sense to me. My inability to find my way doesn't simply extend to the physical world—it means I can barely decipher topographical representations of places I know well. Rand can look at a map and often name the city in question. I see it as a random array of interesting geometric shapes, no more able to inform me of where I am than a painting by Mondrian or Kleé. I hate dystopian stories, and this is a big reason why: I have no skills whatsoever, with the exception of a vast knowledge of European cubists. Unless the rulers of some future postapocalyptic society are art history majors, I'm utterly screwed. The second society crumbles, I'm certain I'll be eaten.

Anyway, the map was utter nonsense. Maps always are.

The island of Manhattan is, for the poetically minded, shaped like the nib of a quill, long and thin, angled sharply at one end. The Bronx buttresses up against it on the north side; Staten Island is just down to the south and west, closer to New Jersey than to Manhattan itself. Just to the east is Queens, with Brooklyn below it, separated from Manhattan by a thin channel of the East River.

I say all this as though I understand it—believe me when I tell you, I do not. Put enough monkeys in front of typewriters, and they will eventually write a novel, albeit one in which the pages are smeared with feces. Alas, I should not judge. Writing a book is difficult.

And there, in that thin sliver of blue water between the boroughs, I saw a tiny strip of land—easily overlooked on my small laminated map—that read "Roosevelt Island." And on it, three rather incredible words: "Smallpox Hospital (Ruins)."

"Yep," I said to myself. "That's it." It's fascinating, the things that move us out of our comfort zones.

Twenty minutes later, after several wrong turns, I was in an aerial tramway that was carrying me away from Manhattan, high over the East River, toward Roosevelt Island. I kept repeating the words that Rand always told me whenever I became frightened of getting irretrievably lost: "You are always just a cab ride away from me."

The first time he said this, I stared at him skeptically.

"What if—"

He knew where I was going. He always does, even if I don't.

"Sometimes it's a very expensive cab ride," he said, delicately cutting me off. "Preceded by a long flight. But I'm still only a cab ride away."

I often whispered this like a mantra, even when I was only wandering a few blocks. And while it was not exactly applicable to Roosevelt Island (it's nearly impossible to find a cab there) the tram ran every fifteen minutes. If it was awful, I could turn around and go back.

The tram swayed. I was thankful that heights were not on my list of many, many fears (moths, pleated front pants, communal showers). I was level with the tops of buildings, watching the interlacing metal of the Queensborough Bridge go by, so close I thought the carriage would scrape it. It was the sort of day that made you feel that the heavens were trying to make amends for some previous meteorological crime. It was 65 degrees and sunny, and the slight wind seemed to carry with it an apology: "I am sorry for the time you sweated through your white dress in the unfettered fury of the sun for twelve full hours on your wedding day. Here's a nice breeze that smells like lemonade."

The tram arrived at the station, and as I took the stairs down and stepped out onto the street, I was hit with that brief moment of panic that I knew so well, the one that accompanies getting lost. *Crap. I don't know where I am, and now I will be eaten.* I always feel that I need to head somewhere with purpose—as though someone is watching and will pounce on me and steal my kidneys when they realize I'm utterly clueless. But there was no one. I'd been in my tram car alone, and there wasn't a soul at the station. There was a bus stop nearby, but the posted fare was only a quarter, and this immediately made me suspicious that it was going to take me straight to Roosevelt Island's premiere human organ–harvesting facility. In reality, it goes to the site of the Pauper Lunatic Asylum, where one of my childhood heroes—investigative journalist Elizabeth Cochran, a.k.a. Nellie Bly—posed as a patient, despite being of completely sound mind. Her exposé on the conditions of asylums and her recommendations for reform would radically change how the mentally ill were treated. True to the New York ethos, the asylum is now a luxury apartment building.

I pulled out my map, and for perhaps the first and only time in my life, found that it was easy to tell where I was, thanks to being across the water from the largest city in America. There was a walkway along the river, and if I followed it far enough, I'd hit the ruins of the Smallpox Hospital.

There is, I realize, no greater example of how maniacal and terrifying the inner workings of my own brain can be than this: having a destination, even if it was the abandoned ruins of an ancient, obviously haunted hospital, was less frightening than not knowing where I was going. At least in this instance, I knew what I was going to encounter: rocks, some bugs, and possibly the disquieted souls of dead children. Better than getting on the wrong train.

I started walking. The path was well maintained at first—clean smooth stone as I headed south and was treated to an unobstructed view of Manhattan's east side. I could still hear the sound of traffic from the island, but it was fainter now—the sound of car horns slightly more muffled, the never-ending hum of thousands of automobile engines fading into white noise. The city was prettier than I'd ever known it to be. Sometimes, in order to see something clearly, you have to step back from it.

I passed some modern buildings, encountered two people sitting on a bench eating their lunch and enjoying the view, and felt entirely at ease. Until I came to the fence.

It extended from the water's edge at my right, across the road and path on which I walked, and disappeared into the growing cluster of thick bramble and trees at my left. Tall, rusted, and menacing, topped with a swirling loop of barbed wire and adorned with a few very clear signs that read "No Trespassing" and "No Loitering." There was a gate that opened where the road was, but it was looped with what appeared to be a slightly thinner iteration of my mother's keychain and padlocked. Just to the right of the gate and directly ahead of me, the fence was further interrupted by a small chain-link door.

It was open.

Funny thing about being constantly scared of getting lost—when you finally know where you're going, you become sort of invincible. Embracing my mother's philosophy of pretty much doing whatever the hell I wanted, I walked through.

I was scared. I was nervous. I was delighted.

I was in the middle of a construction site.

There were huge piles of rock—masonry stones from the original Elmhurst Hospital, which is now in Queens but had once stood here on Roosevelt Island. It had largely served as an overflow facility for Bellevue hospital—and housed asylum, poorhouse, and prisoner patients. The site was quiet.

I kept walking.

The path became narrower as the plants and wildlife began to encroach on it. The smell of pollen and sap and earth grew thicker. I walked down toward the southern tip of the island, and there, just parallel with the Chrysler building across the river, stood the ruins of the Smallpox Hospital.

It's strange where your brain goes when it is fueled by anxiety. Sometimes I feel I'm going to turn into electricity—that I will fizzle and burst and then dissipate into nothing and that will sort of be nice, because then I won't have to worry if I paid the gas bill or not. And sometimes I think about the zombie apocalypse. Obviously.

It's hard to predict what my reaction to a place will be. I've been in utterly tranquil situations, surrounded by people I know and love, and been overcome with anxiety. And I've been in terrifying places—salt mines hundreds of feet underground, abandoned prisons, the state of Florida—and felt completely calm. The Smallpox Hospital should have been scary. But I kept thinking how beautiful it was.

The building itself was reduced to a shell. The façade and the exterior walls remained, but there was no roof and the interior had largely been reclaimed by the original inhabitants of the island—creatures that were small in size and large in number. I could hear them chirping and rustling in the leaves, as the light streamed through and caught the Brownian movement of thousands of particles suspended in the air.

The hospital had been built in the mid-1800s and in its heyday treated seven thousand patients a year. It would eventually become a nurse's dormitory when the island became too populated to house those sick with the virus. It was a Gothic revival of gray stone and arched windows (the panes now long gone) designed by James Renwick, the architect behind St. Patrick's Cathedral on Madison Avenue. Gorgeous, majestic, and by the 1950s, virtually abandoned.

I found it glorious, perhaps in part because of this small and rather incredible fact: it was exactly where I had intended it to be.

And as I sat there looking at it, I found myself doing something else rather out of character. I found myself looking for a gap in the fence *so I could slink through.* The power of knowing precisely where I was had pushed words like "structurally unstable" and "criminal trespass" and "obvious zombie breeding ground" out of my mind. To both my relief and my chagrin, I found no way to get through the fence. My paradoxical mother would have scolded me to no end for even thinking of it. And then she'd wonder why I didn't try to climb over the damn top. I wonder that sometimes, too. I have few regrets in travel, but failing to break into the grounds of the Smallpox Hospital remains one of them.

I was near the southernmost tip of the island now and walked to the end of it—the entire island narrowing to a triangular point. The ground had already been cleared by machinery for the Roosevelt Memorial that would soon be built there. In a year, my little patch of undeveloped forest would be gone. But for now, I was all alone. There was only me and the birds and the entire city of New York.

I listened to the crickets and breathed in the air and then I turned around and headed toward the city. Somehow, on my way back, I ended up in Queens. And you know what? It was *fine.* The heavens did not rain fire and the rivers did not turn to blood and guys in confederate trucker hats didn't suddenly take control of Congress. I simply turned around again and went back to Manhattan.

What that trip hammered home was something I already knew: I was not a travel expert. But I could still travel. I could not speak with authority about places, but I could speak with authority about my experiences. It turned out I was an expert at being me: broken, terrified, and lost. I started writing about what happened when *I* traveled. All the times I'd been led astray, or ripped off, or rendered a nervous, sobbing mess because I needed a snack and someone's airplane-approved therapy pet looked at me weird. I wrote about visiting destinations that weren't really destinations. About hole-in-the-wall restaurants and winding alleys and the poetry written in spray paint on the sides of buildings.

I wrote about Rand, who was always just one cab ride away. I wrote about how he made the world less terrifying simply by being in it. And I wrote about cake.

It was a travel blog, the way I would write it. Messy. Neurotic. And with a surprisingly large number of photos of Jeff Goldblum throughout.

Two years after I started the blog, on a sunny Sunday in Seattle during the summer of 2011, I sat in my pajamas, checking my site traffic as I occasionally do when I want to feel confused. I noticed it had spiked—I had nearly 100 times the visitors I usually did. Curious, I followed the link that was sending me all the traffic and stared blankly at my monitor for a while, trying to suss it all out.

It was a write-up about my blog. The masthead in the corner read *TIME* magazine.

It was their list of the top twenty-five blogs of the year. Rather immediately, I decided that it was some sort of hoax. But as I clicked through the site, I found it looked more and more legitimate, and I grew more and more confused.

I showed it to Rand and asked him if it was real.

"Holy shit, yes. Baby, that's real."

There may have been a little bit of celebratory dancing in our pajamas. I think he picked me up. I think he kissed me. I think he told me I could do anything. I'm speculating here—I don't actually remember, but he tends to do those things on most days.

Looking back, I'm not sure how it happened. I'm guessing the editorial team at *TIME* probably got drunk and thought it was a good idea to include my blog. By the time they sobered up and realized what had happened, it was too late.

They described my writing as "consistently clever," so there's a good chance peyote was involved, too.

The point is, sometimes you have no idea in what direction you're headed, but you keep going anyway. Sometimes, miraculously, you end up in the right place. Sometimes it takes you fifteen years to get there, but you make it. And if you don't? You hop in a cab. If you are lucky, you return with a good story.

I used to be petrified of getting lost. I thought it was a sign that I'd failed. I never realized it might be one of my greatest accomplishments.

5

LIFE LESSONS FROM A THREE-HUNDRED-YEAR-OLD DEAD GUY AND HIS BORING CLOCK

NOT EVERYONE FINDS THEIR MATCH, the variable that solves the equation of their life, the Polaris in the sky that leads them home when they are drunk and jobless and halfway across the globe. I get that. Some people have no interest in finding romantic love. Sometimes, it just doesn't work out. Sometimes a partner seems perfect and then you find out they think *Titanic* was a good movie. The connections we make on this earth are not always what we hope they'd be.

This is one of the few things that my mother and I have in common: my relationship with my father is not what I'd expected. Her relationship with him is not what she'd expected. I figured he'd do fatherly things: ineptly change a diaper, teach me how to ride a bike, and get tearful as I left for college. (Admittedly, I stole most of these ideas from a life insurance commercial. They sound like things dads do, right?) And Mom? Well, she probably expected her marriage to last longer than the Reagan administration.

None of that happened. Dad turned out to be a very different creature than either of us expected. Less sentimental. More serious. Crankier. That's not to say there isn't something valuable in knowing him. You just have to be willing to look. Very, very closely. For *decades*.

My parents were married for eight inexplicable years, four of them spent on separate continents. Mom told me that she knew her marriage was over around the time I was born. No blame was ever assigned to this sentiment, and looking at the two of them now, it's hard to regard their split as anything but inevitable. I was a catalyst, but not the cause—my beginning marked their end.

They separated shortly afterward and divorced when I was four. I don't remember a time when they were ever together, an act of mercy by my infant brain. Imagining them as a couple would be like describing the flavor of violin music.

"Oh, but opposites attract," people often tell me. Yes, they do.

There is something to be said for finding someone who is everything you are not. But my parents are not opposites. Their radical differences do not fall in line in a diametric, corresponding way. We aren't dealing with black and white, with left and right. We are dealing with black and the theory of relativity, with left and a hazy memory from your fifth birthday party.

My father is organized and regimented. He has zero tolerance for nonsense or the unexplained. He likes reading nonfiction, usually about history or war, and he spends a lot of time meticulously constructing highly accurate, fully functional model airplanes. My mother reads book chapters out of order ("I like to skip around") and starts decorating for Halloween in August. Dad's closet is full of several iterations of the exact same shirt, neatly pressed. There is a decent chance my mother is harboring a fugitive in hers.

Rand often talks about what a miracle it is that I am alive at all, explaining that there is nothing more unlikely than the second child of a highly improbable marriage. I try not to question it (if I do, I'm afraid I'll disrupt something in the space-time continuum and will run the risk of disappearing, like Marty McFly almost did in *Back to the Future*). Still, curiosity sometimes gets the better of me, and whenever I ask my mom about those early years of courtship, the answers are less romantic than I would like.

> I don't want to traumatize you.
> It wasn't, like, a bad relationship. Times were different then.
> He kept bringing me coffee.
> I don't know how that happened.
> I think I was depressed.
> Don't write this shit down.

Conclusion: Rand's right. I'm a goddamn miracle. Simply by virtue of *existing* I have achieved something. I often sit around and contemplate this simple but profound truth: I *am*. Then I go eat a piece of cake while still in my pajamas at 3 p.m., because no day is wasted when you are this improbable.

My parents met in Rome while my father was doing work for the US Department of Defense. He and his colleagues in the CIA and US intelligence would hang out in the hotel where my mother worked, across the street from the American embassy. The place was often filled with minor celebrities and oil barons and debutantes, as well as a handful of governmental operatives.

My father's work has always remained murky to us. He told my mother he was a translator for the Department of Defense. She began to suspect that was not the entirety of his role sometime into their marriage when she uncovered a stack of IDs with different names buried deep in his dresser. (It didn't stop either of them from relaying this as my father's profession to my brother and me. As kids, we understood that he had a droll desk job that involved transcription and translation and little else.) In recent years, I've tried to pry stories out of my dad. I get pieces here and there—not enough to paint a full picture, but enough to know that I don't know enough.

My mother always claimed with a measure of pride that back when they first met at the hotel, she always knew exactly what the operatives were up to. My father disagrees. I don't know who is correct, but I wouldn't be entirely surprised if Mom was right: she has always been pretty enough to be a risk to national security. Helen may have launched a thousand ships, but I'm fairly certain Mom played a pivotal if uncredited role in the Cold War.

She was fifteen years his junior; he'd already been married and divorced once, with one son from his previous union—my half-brother, Greg. My parents were married in the consulate in Rome, and the reception was two days later because Dad couldn't get an entire day off work, not even to get married.

I look at their wedding album with the same esteem and wonder one would reserve for a photo of actor Patrick Stewart (a.k.a, Captain Jean-Luc Picard) with a full head of hair—it is concrete evidence of something that shouldn't be. But there they are, standing among the ruins of the Roman Forum, younger than I would ever know them to be. He spoke half a dozen languages and went by half a dozen names. She was the most beautiful woman in Rome. When I think of it in those terms, it almost makes sense.

Soon after they were married, my father was reassigned to his beloved Munich, and so they headed to Germany, where my brother Edward was born. Nearly four years later, Mom left for America while pregnant with me. She said it was because she hadn't enjoyed the birthing process on the military base where my dad was stationed and had heard good things about American hospitals, but I don't think she had any intention of ever returning to Europe.

And so I became the first person in my immediate family to be born in America and one of only three cousins born here.

Dad hung around for a few months, waiting for my mom to be ready to return to Germany, but she never was. Nor was he willing to stay in the United States, when his home and work were in Munich. So he went back to Germany alone.

We saw him once a year for about a month at a time. The visits became less frequent as I got older. I only saw him once between the ages of ten and fifteen, and then again when I was seventeen, and once more when I was nineteen.

I was fairly accepting of his scarcity, as the remoteness seemed in line with my father's temperament. He's doesn't like being close to people either literally or figuratively and isn't particularly sentimental or patient. Neither children, nor teen-agers, nor people in general are his thing.

Once, one of my little cousins made the mistake of throwing his small arms around him in a hug, and he was immediately scared away with a booming "GET OUT."

When I gently chided him for this, he replied, "I didn't like my own children, so why the hell would I like anybody else's?"

This is, I suppose, a rather harsh thing to say to your daughter under any circumstances. But we happened to be in the middle of a dance floor.

At a wedding.

My wedding.

It was during the father-daughter dance, a tradition that I had endeavored to avoid until my father walked up to me and said, "I need to dance with you." I, delighted, told him that I had no idea he had wanted to. "I don't," he said, gesturing to a table of family members, "but they tell me I have to."

Yeah.

Here is the truly remarkable thing: I do not take these things personally. My father was born in the Ukraine during Stalinist rule. On the day before he and his mother and younger brother were supposed to be sent to the gulag, the Nazis took Kiev. In the ensuing shit-show, my grandmother managed to lie low and eventually made her way across Europe with her family. Still in her twenties but already long a widow, she'd be married and widowed again by the end of the war (her second and last husband is where we get our last name). My father's earliest childhood memories are of trekking across a continent at war, of losing two father figures, and of *literally* Hitler.

So, yeah, he's not great at parties.

I've learned to cut him some slack. This isn't how my father treats me. This is how my father treats *life*. His grumpiness is not brought on by circumstance but is simply his constant state of being. For a partial catalog of things that irritate him, you need to simply consult a complete set of unabridged encyclopedias or the entirety of the Internet (which he also hates). There is only one thing he seems to like, though he complains nearly nonstop about it as well—his dog, a snorting, fat little pug named Anton.

Every damn letter he writes to me is filled with talk of that dog. Sometimes he even sends me pictures. Not of Dad and Anton, or my stepmother Margit and Anton, but of *just* Anton.

Therein lay the revelation that as his daughter I so desperately needed: proof that my father can love something and display nothing but vexation for it. He ceased to be as much of an enigma after that. It dawned on me that I had even done a rather brilliant if unintentional impersonation of my father throughout my teen years. I hated everything. Even the things I loved.

This acceptance of mine has been hard-won. Hours spent watching sitcoms during my formative years left me with a clear idea of how fathers should be: kind, caring, inclined to wearing sweater vests, and played by either Michael Gross or Alan Thicke. I wished for a father who didn't get so frustrated with the world. Someone who could accurately be described as kindly and affectionate. Someone who replied to my jokes with something other than "What the hell is wrong with you?"

But that's not my father. And if I kept focusing on what he isn't, I would never see him for what he *is*: honest, if painfully so, brilliant, and generous. Surprisingly easygoing when it came to his expectations of me. He's never demanded love or affection or even a thank you. He's never demanded anything, really, except for an occasional reply to the letters he has sent—and still sends—regularly.

He supported my brothers and me through childhood and college, never grousing about finances. He questions all my small decisions—my clothing, my hairstyles, my choice in reading materials—but never the big ones like my career (specious though it is) or my husband. He expresses his approval with a simple "Fine."

"Dad, I love you."
"Fine."

"Are you and Rand having kids?"
"It doesn't look like it."
"Fine."

And in my father's world, "Fine" is about as good as you can get.

I suppose our relationship is fairly unorthodox, but let's be honest, most relationships are. Besides, it's only ever an issue on Father's Day, when I spend the better part of an hour looking through greeting cards, none of which apply to my dad. Hallmark acknowledges only those fathers who golf or fish, those who are terrible at grilling steaks and spend hours watching professional sports on TV. There are no cards that read, "Thanks for supporting me through college and never directly disputing your paternity."

Which is a shame, because I bet they could make a killing on that one.

It turns out, sometimes you just have to accept people for who they are. Trust me, it's certainly less exhausting. I can spend my time with my dad feeling disappointed, or I can spend it trying to understand the man who was partly responsible for my unlikely existence. It becomes an easy decision when you look at it that way. What is truly remarkable is how very far you will go for that understanding.

* * *

WHEN I WAS IN HIGH school, part of the required reading for one of our classes was a book titled *Longitude: The True Story of a Lone Genius and His Really Fucking Boring Clock* by Dava Sobel.

To be fair, it's been a few years since I've read it, so I might have the author wrong.

I should now, in the interest of coherency, tell you what the book is about. I'm sorry to do this to you.

It's the tale of John Harrison, a British clockmaker who was determined to figure out how to tell a ship's exact location at sea. In the early eighteenth century, seafaring vessels were frequently lost or ended up woefully off course. Annoyed by this, Parliament passed the Longitude Act in 1714, offering twenty thousand pounds (millions of dollars by today's standards) to the first person who could find a method for accurately detecting longitude while at sea to an accuracy of half a degree.

Harrison was convinced that the solution to determining longitude lay in creating a clock that could accurately tell time while at sea.

If I understood the book correctly, this is why creating a working clock was so crucial to figuring out the size of the earth:

In twenty-four hours, the earth spins 360 degrees (this corresponds to the 360 degrees of longitude on a globe). So for every 15 degrees that you move east, the local time moves one hour ahead. For every 15 degrees that you move west, the local time moves back.

Okay, so let's imagine you are on a boat, and it's the seventeenth century (which sounds terrifying. We probably all smell terrible and are about thirty seconds away from dying of scurvy or being burned as witches for knowing how to read. Anyway). Sailors can easily tell the local time from the location of the sun. But in order to know their longitude, they needed to know the time at some distant reference point.

Harrison, brilliant and boring old fool that he was, ended up creating five clocks over several decades—one of which (called the H4) eventually won Parliament's prize. By then Harrison was in his seventies, but he spent the last few years of his life rich, vindicated, and boring.

I suppose, as far as books about clocks go, it's really on the more interesting end of the spectrum, the bar being spectacularly low. And it was quite popular when it came out, because I guess people didn't have a lot else going on in the late 1990s.

But to seventeen-year-old me, it was excruciating.

Every day we'd complain about it, and slowly, I became aware of a trend among the girls in my class: a large number of them had fathers who'd read the book and adored it.

"My dad says it's one of his favorites," my friend Laura told me incredulously one day. "He liked it so much, he lent it to Erin's dad, and he said it's one of the best books *he's* ever read."

Upon hearing this, a rather unexpected and painful pang of longing lodged itself in my throat. I don't get this feeling anymore when I talk to my dad. But when I was younger, it would pop up whenever I was reminded of something I wanted but knew would never happen. In this case, it was the simple back-and-forth between two people, the stories that arose from seeing someone every day.

Weirdly, this hit me harder than any missed birthday parties, softball games, or holidays. I longed for the ability to incorporate my dad into my everyday life—even the most mundane aspects of it. To be able to gesture to some awful book and roll my eyes and say, "Can you believe my old man *liked* it?"

And it was that peculiar longing that caused me to mention that droll little book to my father the next time I was on the phone with him.

"I'm reading this book for class," I said, trying to sound casual, to belie all that I had riding on it, "and it's so, so boring."

Just as I tried to explain what it was about, my father stopped me in mid-sentence.

"I just finished that," he said. "It was fantastic."

And it was at that point that I may have begun to dance around my room, delighted at the wonderful improbability of it all, which left me, like all my friends, bewildered by my father's taste in books.

The next day I would go to class and roll my eyes and say to everyone within earshot, "Oh, god, my dad likes it, too," and it would be wonderful.

I only half-listened as my dad went on about the book's brilliance, twirling around the room until the telephone cord wrapped itself around me and I had to backtrack to unravel it.

Then my father said something that snapped me to attention.

"I gave that book to your brother Greg," he explained. "I told him he had to read it. He thought it was great, too."

My half-brother Greg was, at least during my childhood and high school years, even more of a mystery than my dad. The product of my dad's first marriage, he was more than fifteen years older than me. He'd grown up with his mother in the UK. I'd met him only once.

In the coming years, I would get to know my eldest brother better. I'd learn that we both inherited, along with our brother Edward, a tendency to look sort of pissed-off and squinty in photos, even when we're having a perfectly nice time. Perhaps we aren't that different from our dad after all. Or perhaps it's simply due to our shared Eastern European ancestry—Stalin was burdened with the same expression.

I'd learn that, at over six feet tall, his height was passed down from a mutual grandparent of ours—which sounded nearly unbelievable to me (Edward and I are built like hobbits). I'd discover he was a science geek, that he had an affinity for bad sci-fi films and television shows, and that he was into martial arts. I'd meet his wife, Linda, blonde and petite and absolutely crazy about him. She was already married and had grown children when she met Greg, so my brother went from being single to a step-grandfather on the day they got married, something he told me with no small measure of pride.

He still lives in northern England, and every time he finds out that Rand and I are in London, he tries to make it down or at least calls to say hello. Once, we met in the lobby of our hotel, and he bounded across the room with his enormous strides, lifting me off the ground in a massive hug while yelling, "LITTLE SISTER!"

Sometimes, your relationships with people aren't what you anticipated. Sometimes, they are far, far better.

But when I was seventeen, he was still a mystery, more remote than even my father. And somehow that book—that miserable, dull, wonderful book—had encompassed him, too.

"Your brother Greg even went to Greenwich to see the clock," he said.

"He did what?"

Asking my father to repeat himself is always a risky venture. He will usually do so but with an increase in volume and exasperation. I was fairly certain I'd heard him right the first time— still, I wanted to hear it again.

"HE WENT TO GREENWICH," my father yelled into the phone, "TO SEE THE DAMN CLOCK."

At that precise moment, I made a promise to myself. I was going to take a page from that magnificently droll book our father loved, and I was going to go to Greenwich to see that dreadful clock. I was going to walk the same path that my brother Greg had, and then tell our father about it.

And I was going to love every excruciating minute of it.

My motivations had nothing to do with Harrison's clock. I just wanted to feel a connection to my dad and brother. I wanted the three of us to be tied together by *something* besides our tendency to scowl, and this clock offered me that opportunity. I was determined to make us all part of the same story. Even if it was the most boring story in the damn world.

It would take me a while to get there. Rand's work often brought us to London, but we'd be preoccupied with other obligations or would just be stopping through.

But on a chilly fall day in 2009, deluded by my own sense of determination (and my recent excursion to Roosevelt Island, where I did *not* die), I decided that I would see John Harrison's clock. With singular focus, I marched out of our hotel with my camera, a London Underground pass, and as usual, a dim understanding of precisely where I was going.

Remember: Google had yet to take dominion over the known world. I didn't have GPS tracking or a satellite-enhanced layout of the city—I just had a handful of hastily written directions scribbled on hotel room stationery, which is a daunting prospect for anyone and a potentially disastrous one for me. I considered leaving Rand a goodbye note, decided that was too melodramatic, and instead ate an entire package of cookies the conference organizers had left for him in our hotel room. This gesture would serve as my farewell to the love of my life, in the event that I never made it back.

Supposedly, the clock was in the National Maritime Museum in Greenwich, which, according to their website, is "only 8 minutes by train from London Bridge."

Over the next two hours, this claim would mock me repeatedly.

Despite this boast about how damn close the museum was to central London, I found very few additional directions on the National Maritime Museum's website. It does not help that, for an American, most English addresses are a woefully confusing string of ridiculous phrases and random characters.

Behold:

4 Butthole Lane
Shepshed
Loughborough
Charnwood
Leicestershire
The United Kingdom of Great Britain and Northern Ireland
LE12 9BN

(This is, I kid you not, a *real* address.)

Add a bit of jetlag, and you'll see why I considered it a coup that I managed to make it out of my hotel room.

The maps at the Tube station closest to my hotel were equally unhelpful, but I noticed that the last stop listed for one of the lines was "North Greenwich." Since I knew that the museum was in Greenwich, I figured it was a safe bet to head in that direction.

I will now bestow upon you an important piece of information, one that I did not have before my trip began. North Greenwich and Greenwich are not, in fact, the same place.

Remember that, will you? It will come in handy later.

If you've never traveled on London's subway, it's not unlike being a gerbil run through a maze, except there's no one there to hand you delicious pellets when you go the right way. At least, I don't think there is. I've never done anything but go the wrong way down there, so positive reinforcement has never been a factor.

I took the train from Tottenham Station, transferred at Waterloo (ensuring that the ABBA song of the same name would be stuck in my head for the next three years), and hopped on a second train that would take me to North Greenwich.

I arrived there without incident, which would have been wonderful, had I been in the right place, but the lack of people wearing commemorative "John Harrison's stupid clock" hats soon told me that I was not. I consulted a schematic on a nearby wall and found that once you reach a certain spot on the line, the map changes and suddenly includes a whole bunch of other, previously unlisted stops.

Among them was a stop marked "Greenwich."

To get there, I would need to get back on the line I was on and take it one more stop to Canary Wharf, where I would transfer to something called the DLR. That, eventually, would take me to Greenwich.

Of course, all this was resting on the assumption that the museum was *actually* at the Greenwich stop.

I suppose at this point, it would have been wise and rational to ask someone for help, or buy a proper map, or do anything, really, besides turning around and jumping back on the train from which I'd just stepped off.

But I'd gotten this far without being wise and rational, and it seemed a risky venture to start now. So I climbed back onto my train and took it one more stop to Canary Wharf. The name brought up thoughts of adorable little birds and, phonetically at least, one of my favorite *Star Trek* characters, but let me be the first to share the disappointing news that neither is present in this place.

It is, for the most part, a rather desolate Tube stop in a very corporate area. I walked through it, looking for the connection to the DLR, which I soon found out stood for "Docklands Light Railroad," a train service whose official slogan is, I'm fairly certain: "Located nowhere near Canary Wharf."

I walked across several long plains of cement, looking for the DLR. There was not a soul in sight, and as I wandered, I started to wonder, as I often do. What would happen if I never made it back home? Is there irony in losing time to search for a clock?

Just as my worries began to reach a fever pitch, I caught sight of the DLR stop and was able to catch the next train. My confidence was renewed.

That feeling lasted for approximately ninety seconds, until a voice over the PA system announced that the car I was presently sitting in needed to be repaired, and we had to vacate it at the next stop.

Really? NOW? It couldn't make one more stop without falling apart?

At this point, I was beginning to suffer the sort of break with reality that happens to all tourists, that causes us to think that paying $18 for a gelato is totally reasonable, or that we really, really need a foam cheddar top hat.

It was in this fragile state that I stepped off the train and watched it lurch on, empty, as I and a few other poor souls stood stranded at a wayward, aboveground stop.

Do you remember that part of *Return of the Jedi* where Vader tells Luke that he's his father and chops off his hand? (My apologies if I just included a decades-old spoiler there, but seriously, what have you been doing with your life?) And Luke's just dangling off of some piece of metal at the bottom of Cloud City, and the audience sort of collectively thinks, "Welp, you're screwed, Skywalker. That is not a highly trafficked area."

It felt a little like that.

By the time the replacement train slid up to the station, I was somewhat delirious. I took it to Greenwich.

Which was not the right stop.

Turns out that the museum is actually at Cutty Sark, which is directly before the Greenwich stop. There is an incredibly useful map that indicates this (and even includes a cute little icon with a tiny boat on it) but, for reasons that totally escape me, it is only posted *at* Greenwich and not before. It's a charming way of saying, "Congratulations, you cocked up."

So I found the DLR heading in the opposite direction, went back the way I came, and got off at Cutty Sark, a shell of the person I once was.

There were, conveniently, signs everywhere indicating that I was in the right place.

I stopped by a small bakery and got a snack, a preemptive move against any low-blood-sugar-induced crying fits, and asked the man behind the counter where I could find the museum.

"Just follow that road," he said, pointing at an unspecific path in the distance. "You can't miss it."

I very much wanted to grab the front of his shirt and hiss, "Sir, you have no *idea* how easily I can miss things."

Instead, though, I just nodded and took a bite of my focaccia, which was excellent.

Miraculously, he was right about the path in addition to making totally decent bread. I followed the road he'd indicated, turned a corner, and there it was: the National Maritime Museum. The building was massive, white, and stately, with enormous columns in front and giant anchors flanking the wide walkway to the front door. It was a lovely place, I thought, for Harrison's clock to reside.

I walked through the front doors and found an information desk behind which a pleasant-looking older woman sat.

"Could you please direct me to John Harrison's clock?" I asked, trying my best to conceal both my excitement and exhaustion at the odyssey that had led me there.

"Oh, I'm afraid it's not here," she said.

Now, I suspect that in the history of Maritime Museums, there have been relatively few instances when a guest has become entirely unhinged and has gone around smashing exhibits, kicking interactive displays, and making some very graphic threats involving sextants, but there, on that day, I came very, very close.

The woman must have read my expression—a mix of incredulity, disappointment, and constipation (after all, we'd been in London for a few days by then)—and quickly explained that the clock was located not far from where we were, at the Royal Observatory.

"You can't miss it," she said.

Exhausted, I roamed around the museum for a bit. It has all manner of objects and artifacts pertaining to British Naval History. (It mostly tells the story of old white men in boats. If you can't make it there, don't fret. There are 286 other museums in the UK that focus on this exact same topic. Seriously.) I wandered around for twenty minutes or so before the realization hit me that I could, indeed, miss it: I had no idea when the observatory closed.

Petrified that I'd have traveled all this way only to meet a locked door, I ran out the front doors and up the adjacent hill, at the top of which stood the Royal Observatory and, supposedly, Harrison's clock. But all this was hypothetical: at this point in time, I believed nothing and trusted no one.

The hill was deceptively steep, and I rushed up it so quickly, I noticed that a few heads turned as I passed. I looked like someone who needed astronomy, very urgently.

I reached the top, gasping for air. I was there. After two hours and numerous trains and not nearly enough of an intake in calories, I had arrived. And just in time, too. I paid my admission and reached the front door just as a guided tour was beginning—the only one of the day. I stood sweaty and disbelieving my timing could have been so perfect.

Everyone had been right. I couldn't miss it.

The guide, a blonde woman with a square jaw and twinkling eyes, seemed genuinely delighted with her work. We began in the courtyard out front, which was bisected by a line laid into the cement—the Prime Meridian. This was the home of Greenwich Mean Time.

She led us into Flamsteed House—a large, tawny, brick structure, with a dome observatory in the center of its roof and told us the history of the building. Parts of it dated back to 1675; it was built by order of King Charles II. One massive octagonal room had been designed with the express purpose of observing astronomical events and planetary movement, but it was never used as such. The builder had failed to align any of the walls with a meridian, making positional observation impossible from its vantage point.

It was in this lovely and useless place that she told us the history of John Harrison. It had been more than a decade since I'd read the story, but I was amazed at how many of the gloriously boring details came back to me. How Harrison had created five timepieces in total, and how the second-to-last one—the H4, as it was called—kept extraordinary accuracy, running slow by less than a second over the course of an entire day. How the Board of Longitude kept insisting that the success of Harrison's clock was a fluke and refused to pay him the reward money. How they kept the H4 for so long that Harrison got fed up and built a fifth and final clock. How the king himself eventually stepped in and awarded the prize to Harrison, who by then was in his seventies.

Every. Boring. Detail. It all came rushing back. I hadn't felt that sort of wonder and ennui since I was seventeen.

At the end of the tour, we entered a small gallery, and there he was on the wall—or a portrait of him, at least—the same one that had graced the cover of my schoolbook all those years before.

And even further in were all of Harrison's clocks. The early iterations, giant rectangular contraptions of gears and springs and cogs, looking like Industrial Revolution–era cuckoo clocks. And lastly, I saw the H4, the clock that won the Longitude Prize, humbly resting in a glass case. For reasons of preservation, it was not wound but was perfectly still and silent.

That fucking clock. It was just *sitting* there.

After such a long, strange trip, I suppose our meeting could only have been uneventful. Unsure of whether to laugh or scream, I took out my camera, and despite the many, many signs to the contrary, I snapped a few surreptitious photos before I was scolded by a security guard and pretended not to understand English.

And then I left.

The trip back to the hotel was relatively short. I almost knew where I was going and at no point did my train randomly stop, leaving me stranded in some forgotten corner of outer London. I dozed a little, jet lag finally catching up with me, and I managed not to miss my stop.

As I walked backed to the hotel, I found that my mood had fallen with the denouement of my adventure. I shouldn't have felt disappointed—I'd gone looking for a clock, and I'd found one. The problem was that I wasn't as impermeable as I'd imagined. I'd inadvertently forged the belief that somehow, upon seeing the clock, the piece of my life that was my father would fall into place. That he would be transformed into some-one happy and affectionate who wore sweater vests if I just tried hard enough and went far enough and looked at that clock long enough. That once I made my pilgrimage, he'd be transformed into someone he was not, someone he could not be.

It was the same lesson that I'd been struggling with all along: I needed to accept things for what they were. The clock wasn't there to fix my life or to heal the longing that resided in my throat any more than falling in love could cure depression or give me six-pack abs. It's a *clock*. If you demand more of it than that, you will invariably be disappointed.

Ultimately, I was able to regard it for what it was: a rather remarkable invention in its own right. It had helped detect true longitude and changed the way humans circumnavigated the globe. This clock helped travelers find their way. When viewed in that light, it was nothing short of incredible.

Later than evening, I met up with Rand and some friends of ours. They asked me about my day, and I told them the saga of the subway, of my father and John Harrison and that wonderful, horrible clock. And as I sat there, obviously boring them with ir-relevant details about ancient timepieces, it occurred to me that the thing I'd wanted since I was a teenager—to have my father be part of the mundanity of my everyday life—had happened. In that instant, he wasn't remote or distant. He had been the catalyst for my travels across London, for my being haunted by a timepiece for a decade and a half.

In light of this, when I was asked whether the clock was worth seeing, my answer was an unequivocal yes. For me, it cer-tainly had been worth it.

"You just have to accept it for what it is," I said.

If you do that, you'll never be disappointed.

6

YOU TAKE THE GRENADE MY MOM BROUGHT TO DINNER; I'LL BOOK OUR FLIGHT—FINDING BALANCE IN RELATIONSHIPS

NONE OF IT WOULD HAVE happened—not the blog, not the family connections, not my pitiful but still valiant attempt at understanding cardinal directions—without Rand. It's no surprise he was the one who gave me the guiding ethos to make me less afraid of travel, and of the world in general. He brought a sort of harmony to my life that wasn't there before. I don't really remember what things were like without him. When I try to think of it, I mostly picture screaming and burning buildings and wild dogs.

He taught me that a good relationship requires balance. A certain give-and-take between two people who find that the world makes more sense when they are together than when they're apart. When I perform autopsies on my failed love af-fairs, it becomes apparent that balance was missing.

A lot of other things were missing, too. Empathy. Patience. A shared understanding of what the word "monogamy" means.

Then I met Rand. He is the perfect counterpoint to all that I am.

As you may have gathered by now, I am not a calm per-son. If I ever look distracted, it is because I am planning out an escape route in case whatever building I am in spontaneously combusts, or I'm looking for something to cling to in the event that gravity suddenly reverses itself. At times I am neither ratio-nal nor logical because fear and anxiety have taken over. It's as if my brain is a frightened, angry baboon. You cannot get the ba-boon to relax, because it will lunge for your jugular. You do not tell it to calm down, because baboons do not tend to understand English. Instead, you give it a snack, and if you have enough presence of mind, you lace said snack with THC. And then you carefully back away.

Stoned baboon is the best we can hope for.

I am a neurotic worrier. I obsess about things. I hold grudges. I'm basically Larry David, if he were raised by Don Corleone from *The Godfather*. (Just when I think I'm out . . . I need to run back inside and make sure I didn't leave the iron on.) If I married someone like me, our tombstone (after years of nervous, panicked marriage) would read: "DID YOU RE-MEMBER TO PAY THE ELECTRIC BILL?"

Fortunately, Rand is different. He shrugs things off, and he's perfectly happy smiling brightly at unpleasantness. He forgives and loves and rarely worries. He's almost reckless in his desire to not stress the details in his personal life. That said, when it

comes to work, he is almost as crazy as I. We all have our weak-
nesses. His is a software startup.

I can count on two hands the number of times I've seen him
actually lose it. It tends to be when freaking out is entirely called
for, but I am unable to muster the reserves of energy required
to do it because after three decades of being entirely unhinged
I need a nap. The first time it happened was the year my mother
came over for Easter dinner, and I was exhausted from having
spent the day cleaning and cooking and having imaginary preemptive fights with my family. By the time Mom opened up her
purse and said, "You will not believe what I found," and then
pulled out a perfectly spherical World War I–era grenade, *which
she was holding up by the pin*, I could only stare blankly at it.

"Huh," I said.

This was one of the rare moments when Rand took over the
noble role of screaming at my mother.

"IOLANDA WHAT THE HELL! PUT THAT DOWN!"

"What? It's just a grenade. It doesn't work anymore," she
said assuredly. She held it upside down to reveal a hole in the
bottom, presumably where the explosives went, and to her
credit, they did appear to be gone. After all, Mom's not completely irresponsible. If she brings a grenade into your home, it
probably won't be live.

"Oh, it doesn't work," I repeated, calmly.

"You don't know that. NONE OF US KNOW THAT,"
Rand shouted, which was a fair point. I started dicing some
shallots for a salad.

"We need to get rid of it," he said.

Mom's reaction was, unsurprisingly, not in accordance with
this.

"Nooo," she whined. "Why do we need to throw it out?"

"Because *it is a grenade*."

"I'll keep it then," she said.

My husband, having learned that the process of fighting with my mother is roughly as effective as screaming at the ocean to be less watery, acquiesced. His compromise: she could keep the grenade, but not in the house. Rand gingerly took it from her, demanded her car keys, and walked cautiously out the front door.

"Don't throw it out!" Mom called after him.

"I AM PUTTING IT IN THE TRUNK OF YOUR CAR BEFORE ANYONE ELSE GETS HERE," he yelled back, while taking small, metered steps away from us.

My mother pouted. She had been excited about the grenade because it was visually similar to an Easter egg, she explained, and had decided that it would therefore be a perfect gift on a day when we were celebrating the resurrection of Christ. She thought it was neat and wanted us to have it.

I nodded. It was all rather sweet if you didn't think about it too much.

Rand came back a few minutes later, short of breath and clutching his heart, a move he learned from me. My mother began to defend her actions. Rand cut her off.

"Iolanda, no. Just . . . thank you, it's very sweet . . . but no. No grenades. I'm sorry," he said, and then excused himself to go upstairs for a few moments, presumably to weep.

"What wrong with Rand?" Mom asked.

I shrugged.

"He has a weird thing about grenades or something," I said. And then I put out some hummus and carrot sticks and went to check on dinner.

This is a man who will scream and lose his mind with worry on my behalf when I am too exhausted to do so. Thankfully, the rest of the time, I've got it down.

On nights before early morning flights, I've seen him set the alarm clock for p.m. instead of a.m. on more than one occasion. When I catch his potentially disastrous error (and I always do, because part of being me requires checking the alarm clock a half dozen times or so before bed) and point it out to him, he just laughs and says something like, "Well, it's a good thing I have you."

That's the thing I never realized before I met him: for the longest time, I was looking for someone to make sense of my life. I never imagined that I would help him make sense of his.

I don't think this is unique to us. I think the entire planet operates the same way, possibly the entire universe. For every action, there's an equal and opposite reaction. For every straight man, there's a prankster. For every me, there's a Rand.

I don't mean to suggest that there's one person out there whom we are meant to be with. We live on a rather densely populated planet—there are lots of people with whom you could potentially share your time. But I think that only a select few of them can help put the disparate pieces of your life perfectly into place. And when that happens, the universe sighs happily, because it, too, has achieved a sort of balance.

He taught me to relax. To be less afraid of travel and less afraid of everything, really. When our luggage was stolen in San Francisco during a weekend trip, he picked me up and said, calmly, "I will fix this." When I lost my job he told me, confidently, that things would be fine. When I accidentally flambéed bananas in a fireball that threatened to burn down the first apartment we ever shared together, he screamed really loudly but then helped me put out the flames.

I feel constantly indebted to him for making my life better. Every now and then, I'm able to return the favor. It's few and far between, but it happens—as it did on the night when we should have been in Paris.

* * *

IT WAS JUNE 2011—that same wonderful summer during which my blog had started to really take off. His company and his speaking engagements continued to grow, and it felt like maybe he and I were starting to figure out what the hell we were doing. It was only fair that the universe push us around a little.

Rand was scheduled to keynote a conference in the city of light, and it would be our very first time there, save for a few exhausted connections made at Charles de Gaulle Airport, which I would easily write off as one of the worst in the world were it not for one saving grace: macarons. Macarons everywhere.

Ours was an afternoon flight, and the day had been sunny and clear and lovely in a way that is unheard of for Seattle at that time of year. June in the Pacific Northwest is often a miserable affair, but we accept it because we know that what follows will be a glorious July, and then the best August in the country.

After the gloom of June has passed, the cloudless, sunlit days reach 75 degrees. Mount Rainier, snow-capped and giant, looms in the south, Puget Sound shimmers blue, and the city is—for a brief window of time—stunningly beautiful. The sun stays out until late, traces of light remaining in the sky until well past 10 p.m. The temperature drops 20 degrees at night, and the next day, it happens all over again. Two whole months of perfect days.

So we've learned not to expect too much of June, and we're okay with that trade-off.

But this day in June was different. It was as though we'd died and gone to Southern California. We waited in the sunshine for our cab to arrive and take us to the airport. Over my arm I'd tossed my raincoat: the forecast for Paris was not promising.

Before any flight, a cluster of butterflies will emerge from some chrysalis hidden in my body and flock to my stomach. I clutched my gut as we rode to the airport. The anxiety had begun.

I am not a nervous flyer. But I am a nervous check-in-and-get-through-security-er. Everything that happens right up until the cabin door closes is enough to panic me: there is so very much that can go wrong. You could get delayed in security, or find yourself in line behind a serial farter, or discover that your mother has left a miniature pickax in her bag.

I know, I know: there is plenty that can go wrong after a flight takes off, but that's never bothered me all that much. Maybe I realize that if something goes awry at 30,000 feet, there's nothing I can do about it. Maybe I always think I'm on the verge of dying anyway, so being in a plane isn't significantly more dangerous than petting a cat (my Auntie Pia swears you can catch bubonic plague from cats). Whatever the reason, I don't fear flying. Just everything else.

This day was no different and was made all the worse because we were flying on Air France. There is, I am almost certain, no airline that can make the whole process of getting on board more difficult.

For some reason, we were unable to check in online. This, in the world of literature, is what is known as foreshadowing. And so my husband and I were forced to speak to someone who worked at the ticketing counter at Air France.

We found ourselves, rather shockingly, dealing with an agent who was quite pleasant and helpful. I suspect she no longer works for the airline, because there was no way she was going to make it very far at that company with an attitude like that. She was young, with a bright smile and a low ponytail of thick brown hair. In what I can only assume is a brilliant preemptive measure against customer service complaints, I noticed that she and everyone else behind the counter lacked name tags.

So I will call her June, because that's what month it was and because there aren't enough Junes in the world, of either variety.

We waited patiently as June, too, was unable to find our reservation. This wasn't particularly surprising, as I am fairly certain AF handles all ticketing information through an elaborate system of Post-It notes, but it was rather stressful. I felt my blood pressure climb steadily upward as Rand used his phone to scroll through his email, looking for some clues as to why our reservation had vanished.

Now, let me take a moment here to provide you with a little background on Air France.

It is the worse airline in the world. In order to work there, you do not need to be a self-motivated worker or an independent thinker. You do not need to thrive in stressful, fast-paced environments. Their only criteria for hiring seems to be a thorough and prevailing disgust with humanity, a loose understanding of what planes are, and a deep-rooted disdain for linear time.

All of that being said, I do admire their commitment to hiring sociopaths and xenophobes, because hey, they need to make a living, too. I just wish that fewer of them worked in customer service.

Rand continued to scroll through his email until he stopped with a start. June, on the other side of the counter, was oblivious to us as he whispered, "Oh, god," under his breath.

"What?" I asked.

Slowly, he turned his phone toward me.

On the small screen was our flight confirmation email, sent by Air France, with all the details of our trip to Paris. We were in the Premium Voyageur cabin, one teeny but nevertheless glorious step up from Economy (which is, on most transatlantic flights, a surprisingly accurate recreation of a nineteenth-century debtor's prison).

There were our names, our passport information, our seats, and times of departure. Everything looked in order, until I scanned the date. Friday, June 3.

Which would have been totally fine had it not been Saturday, June 4.

"Our flight was yesterday," Rand whispered, his eyes wide and disbelieving.

I tilted my head toward June, who was unsuccessfully trying to locate our reservation.

"You cannot tell her," I hissed back. Not my proudest moment, sure, but I can explain my actions thus:

1. I'm not a very good person.
2. As long as June believed that Air France had erred, we still had a chance of getting on that flight. Thus far, it

seemed like a good one, too: she'd found evidence of the transaction. Clearly, the tickets had been paid for— there was just no date.

3. I wasn't entirely sure it wasn't Air France's fault. They were capable of some pretty exceptional bureaucratic incompetence. I'd flown on the airline and nearly missed connections because they had us arrive at a gate *whose door to the main terminal was locked.* Imagine an entire plane of people, ripe from an international flight, locked in a hallway for half an hour until someone noticed. Then having to run across the hellscape that is Charles de Gaulle Airport because if we missed our next flight, Air France would not reimburse us because *technically we'd landed on time.*

4. I'm starting to think my relationship with Air France is like Harry Potter's with Voldemort. Long ago there was a prophecy that I would ruin them, and they've been trying to destroy me ever since.

Okay, fine, it was *technically* our fault, and given Rand's penchant for setting his alarm clock wrong, I felt more than marginally responsible for not double-checking the flight details.

I was thoroughly content to keep the truth of our mix-up to ourselves. I mean, some people keep entire secret families on the side. And to my knowledge, neither Rand nor I have those (*though how would we know?*), so really, this seemed like not that big a deal.

But my husband is, to a fault, unwaveringly honest—just another one of those things about him that brings balance to my life. There was no way he was keeping this to himself, and despite my suggestions to the contrary, he immediately told June what had happened.

"I need to be in Paris by Monday morning," Rand said. This was one of the few times in my life, besides our interactions with my mother, when I could hear panic in his voice. He was delivering the opening keynote session for a conference of several thousand marketers.

June was clearly new on the job, because she still seemed to have a modicum of affection for her fellow humans. She quickly set about finding Rand another ticket while my husband began to take short, panicked breaths. I gently took his face in my hands.

"It's gonna be okay," I said, my voice calm in a way that it never is. I'm nervous when I'm *sleeping*. But seeing that this time, it was Rand who needed to panic, I suddenly was able to summon it up from somewhere. If he was going to freak out, I could shrug it off. Balance.

"I can't believe this," he said, running his hands through his hair.

"It's gonna be okay. But if you can't get to Paris, is there someone who can fill in for you?"

Rand squeezed his eyes shut and nodded. "Maybe. Yeah. I have to make a few phone calls."

"Why don't you go do that," I said, smiling. "I've got this."

Who was this calm, reasonable person I had briefly become? And why was she never, ever around during my family get-togethers or reality show finales?

I stayed at the counter as June tapped at her keyboard and squinted at the screen in front of her.

"Two tickets, right?"

"No. At this point, one is fine, too. If possible, in the same cabin that we were in," I said. I was okay with staying home, if it meant that Rand didn't have to fly economy. He suffers from a degenerative disc disease, a condition that is, in his case, painful and permanent, so long flights are not kind to him. A few extra inches of legroom make a huge difference.

"Oh," I added, "and if it's affordable, that would be awesome."

June smiled. "I'll see what I can do."

I liked her.

As she toiled away at her station, I noticed that another Air France employee had appeared, standing a few feet away, watching us. Her blonde, much-abused hair was pulled tightly away from a face that seemed most comfortable wearing a resolute scowl. She seemed to hold some measure of seniority, presumably achieved by drinking the sacrificial blood of kittens.

"Okay, got two in Premium Voyageur!" June announced brightly. At that moment, the woman who'd been watching us swooped in. She spoke directly into June's ear, without a glance at me or the screen.

"Do not give her that one."

June started and turned sharply to look at her, but she'd already retreated back to where she was.

"Um . . . " I said, which I felt summed up the situation well.

"Okaa-aay," she said, "apparently I can't give you that seat."

"No problem," I replied, brightly, tapping a reserve of optimism and patience that had remained well hidden for the last thirty or so years. "Let's try for another one."

June continued typing away.

"Alright! I found you another one."

And again, the woman from before swooped in.

"Not that one."

June's brow wrinkled.

"Is there a reason that—" she began.

"Do *not* sell her that seat."

At this point, I noticed an agent at an adjacent desk peer over to June's monitor and back at the supervisor. Clearly, the woman's decrees made no sense to anyone. She was taking a weird pleasure out of making life difficult for June. And for me.

I decided not to give her any satisfaction from seeing me rattled.

"OKAY!" I said, brightly and just a little too loudly. "Let's give it another shot."

June found another seat. And once again her supervisor swooped in. We were not allowed that one, either. June began to protest.

"But it's an unsold seat! Why can't I—"

"NO," she snapped. I swear, I saw a small smile play on her lips, as she retreated back to where she had been standing. A peculiar little power play was taking place.

I took a deep breath, closed my eyes, and when I opened them, I found I was smiling.

"Fourth time's the charm, right?" I said. I'd clearly gone insane. It was kind of fun.

June nodded, but she was clearly rattled.

"Um, there's nothing left in Premium Voyageur. I mean, there is," she said, lowering her voice and gently inclining her head towards her supervisor, "but she says I can't sell them to you."

"Let's try economy, then. Preferably an aisle."

More clicking. More waiting. Rand returned, somewhat frazzled. He'd managed to get his friend Will, in London, on the phone. If worst came to worst, could he be in Paris on Monday morning, ready to deliver a presentation that he'd never seen before to a few thousand people?

Yes. Of course.

Knowing that Will could fill in calmed Rand down a bit, but he was still on edge. He didn't want to make his friend rush off to Paris for his own oversight.

"Okay," June said, "I found you an aisle seat!"

And guess what happened when she announced that. Go ahead. Guess. That's right: THE SUPERVISOR STOPPED HER AGAIN.

"Wait, what?" Rand said. "Why can't I—"

"Not. That. One," the supervisor said, and walked off. By now, we'd attracted the attention of the other ticketing agents, and a few passengers. People were exchanging looks with one another.

Rand stared at me, his mouth half open.

"What the hell is going on?" he asked.

"Psychological experiment," I whispered, and turned back to June.

"Shall we try again?" I said. Then I smiled brightly and, catching the supervisor's eye, gave her a little wink. This did not improve the situation.

June nodded. At this point, I think she had something to prove. A few minutes later, she found us another seat, and, rather wisely, whispered her findings to me.

"I found another seat—but it's a window."

"That's fine," I said, and handed her my credit card. I looked around—the woman had been called away.

I kept my voice low.

"Since she's gone, is there any way you could upgrade him to Premium Voyageur?"

"Um . . ."

"There are seats available, right?"

June nodded. "Yeah," she said and tilted her head over where the woman had stood, "but she doesn't want me to give you them. And if she finds out I did . . ."

She frowned at me, nervously. Understood. This was June's career we were talking about. We'd been terrorized by her supervisor for a few moments. She dealt with it every day.

"It's cool," I said.

I turned to Rand.

"Babe, you're going to Paris alone. In economy. If you make it through alive, you might be stronger for it. But odds are you will return a sad and broken man."

I handed him the ticket June had just printed.

We began to leave—I was going home, Rand was going to Paris, a day late, and many, many dollars short.

"STOP."

It was June's supervisor.

"Now, what?" Rand snapped.

"You need to weigh your bag," she said.

"I already *did*," Rand said. This was true. When we'd first arrived, June had placed the bags on the scale. Everything was fine.

"You need to weigh it again."

Rand stared at me. I shrugged. There could be no harm, right? It wasn't as though his bag had gotten heavier while we'd been standing there.

"Just weigh it again," I said, gently patting his forearm.

Rand placed his carry-on back on the scale.

"It's too heavy," she said. "You'll need to check it."

I feel it pertinent to note that Rand had a specific fear of checking his bag on Air France, and for good reason: the airline doesn't remotely care if your bag arrives or not. On one return flight from Europe, we checked our bags, only to find that Rand's (and not mine) was inexplicably left behind at Charles de Gaulle Airport because, to the best of our understanding, the baggage handler loading the plane didn't like the color of it.

Of course, no one told us this, and so we were left standing at the baggage claim in Seattle, patiently waiting for a bag that never arrived. We finally went to the counter to see what had happened and they snapped at us.

"We've been paging you for twenty minutes," they said, exasperated. This was a vicious lie. I'd been listening very closely to the PA. They had not been paging Rand Fishkin. They'd been paging an individual by the name of Flopsy Bugmittens.

So, naturally, Rand was a little nervous to check his bag again. Especially when it met the weight restrictions.

"No," he said, firmly.

"Excuse me?" the supervisor asked. This, I realized, is what she'd been waiting for.

"I'm not checking my bag," Rand said, and he started to walk away.

"THEN YOU AREN'T GETTING ON THE FLIGHT!" she yelled.

I'd like to think that even Gandhi lost his temper now and again. That for all his nonviolence and passive resisting, there was one thing that could make him positively lose it. Like someone leaving just one tiny, unusable scrap of toilet paper on the roll in the bathroom, so that they didn't have to change the whole roll.

Everyone has their hot buttons. Things that infuriate them, regardless of how calm and understanding a nature they usually possess.

And for Rand, the thing that causes him to totally lose it, even more so than bringing a hand grenade to Easter dinner, is a senseless abuse of power. Also, having to check his bag.

"FINE," he said.

The woman smiled, satisfied.

"Fine, you'll check your bag?"

"No," Rand said. "I'm not getting on the flight."

I really wish I had had my camera out, because the expression on her face would have made for an awesome, if confusing, Christmas card.

"Babe," I said, gently. "Are you sure?"

He nodded. "This is insane."

I walked up to June and handed her my credit card again.

"Can you please refund our most recent ticket purchase?"

She nodded.

All eyes were on us now, and I suspect the supervisor had realized that she'd gone too far. In a blink, she disappeared through a rear door.

"Crap," Rand said. "I have to call Paris."

I nodded and sent him off. It was now just June and me. I told her how much I appreciated her help and thanked her profusely.

"But your supervisor is a sadist," I said. "And I need to know her name so I can file a complaint."

June nervously looked over her shoulder, and, sure that no one was watching, smiled slightly as she told it to me.

It's been years since these events transpired. To share her name with you now would be petty and childish.

It was Elizabeth.

She is five feet three inches or so, with dishwater blonde hair. My memory fails me, but I think her eyes were either blue or blood red. If you are flying Air France out of Seattle-Tacoma International Airport, I recommend that you pack some holy water in your bag should you encounter her. Be sure to make it less than three ounces, TSA restrictions being what they are.

A few minutes after Elizabeth disappeared, we left as well. Rand and I stood on the curb outside the airport, enjoying the sun, and feeling not all that disappointed about not being in Paris. Will had graciously agreed to deliver Rand's presentation for him—and it turned out he was fluent in French, to boot. So the Paris conference-goers had to suffer through an informative and entertaining presentation delivered by a devastatingly hand-some Brit.

"What now?" Rand asked. I smiled. I knew exactly where we were going.

Being on the road as much as we are, we miss a lot of things. Birthdays, weddings, baby showers, the occasional bris. On that particular night when we should have been traveling to Paris, our friend Jamie was having a birthday party.

I've found that, proper etiquette aside, when you RSVP "no" to a party and then show up unexpectedly, people are often de-lighted to see you. It helps, of course, if they are already drunk, you are wielding two dozen cupcakes, and there is a story to be told.

The Mandarin Gate Chinese Restaurant and karaoke bar sits in a strip mall in North Seattle, just off Aurora Avenue. A mile south is the rather affluent neighborhood of Green Lake, and a mile west lies Carkeek Park, with its sweeping views of Puget Sound. But the stretch of highway where Mandarin Gate is located is known mostly for easy access to drugs, prostitution, and venereal disease.

It is not, one could safely say, the most romantic of places.

Nor can I speak to the quality of food served at the establishment. The drinks, judging by the quantity consumed and the presumed buying power of the clientele, are affordable and the pours are generous.

The back bar, which is open long after the kitchen has closed, is a sea of white linoleum and chipped paint, all bathed in the soft glow of the rainbow Christmas lights that hang limply from the walls. At one end of the room sits a small but inviting stage.

On the night when we should have been in Paris, we found ourselves here, celebrating our friend's birthday, along with a cast of people who I presumed were Mandarin Gate regulars, seated at the bar, their backs to the room. At the center of all this Rand and I sat, surrounded by friends, eating cupcakes and trying to explain why we were still in Seattle.

People would occasionally rise from the table, either alone or with a conspirator, whenever their names were called, and head toward the small stage.

Depending on the song, we'd sit and watch and cheer, or sing along, or get up and dance.

At some point, our friend Sarah took the stage. Standing up there, her blonde hair floating around her as she moved back and forth, belting out perfect notes, it might as well have been Broadway.

Except that she was singing the Smiths.

It was a song I loved, a song I listened to constantly around the time I first met Rand. Every now and then, when we're flying and hitting a spot of turbulence, I hear the lyrics in my head and take his hand.

> *And if a double decker bus*
> *crashes into us*
> *to die by your side*
> *is such a heavenly way to die.*

I suppose it's easy to see why the tune appealed to my sensibilities. I can't escape my worries. The bus is always barreling down toward us. Rand sees it, too, but rather than panic, he tells me that everything will be okay, and I start to believe it. He might be wrong, but he's usually right. Either way, he's there, by my side.

As Sarah sang, perfectly and dramatically and to the delight of everyone in that back bar, I found myself next to Eric, her husband of less than a year. And as he looked at her, he smiled and said to no one in particular, "That is *my* wife."

I think about that moment often. And about the countless other moments I'd missed while I was frantically running off somewhere. Eric plays his cards close to the vest, and it's only if you pay very close attention that you see exactly how in love he is with my dear friend. I was the only one that heard him say those words that night. Had I been in Paris, maybe no one would have.

One by one, the regulars at the bar came alive and walked up to the stage.

Then came Richard. He'd been sitting quietly at the bar since we'd arrived. He was middle-aged and barrel-chested, his white hair slicked back against his head. Upon hearing his name, he stood, grabbed his sports jacket off the back of his chair, and shrugged it on. And as he passed our table, straightening his lapel, he winked at me.

In a few moments, he was channeling Barry White, belting out "Can't Get Enough of Your Love, Babe" with such a booming resonance that the walls shivered. Rand took my hand and walked me to the makeshift dance floor at the center of the bar. As we swayed in the pink light, he glanced at his watch.

"Our plane just landed at Charles de Gaulle," he said.

I laughed and pulled him close.

"I do so love Paris in springtime," I said.

He immediately began to apologize.

"I'm so sorry," he said. "I can't believe I lost it like that."

"It's cool," I replied. "That woman was nuts."

"She *was*. How on earth did you stay so calm?"

I shrugged.

"It was just my turn, I guess."

The instances are few and far between, but every now and then, he and I are given the chance to switch roles. When life becomes just a little bit too much for him, in a way that it almost never does, I remember all the comforting things he's said to me, and I repeat them to him. I look at the bus that is heading straight for us and I tell him, calmly, that everything will be fine. I make things right. For a brief moment, I get to be the best person I know. I get to be Rand. And he, poor fool, has to be me.

It has to be that way. If you both panic, you'll both be miserable. And if no one does, you end up with explosives at Easter Sunday dinner. It is the law of the conservation of matter and Newton's third law of physics. It is what holds the planets in orbit around the sun.

The night that we should have been in Paris, we were in a karaoke bar in North Seattle, dancing under rainbow Christmas lights and helping to keep the universe in perfect balance.

7

MARRY SOMEONE WHO WILL HELP YOU DEAL WITH YOUR SHIT

MISSING THAT FLIGHT TO PARIS taught me something important: you don't even need to set foot on an airplane to have an epiphany about your relationships. You can learn a lot about someone without going anywhere. Some of my biggest revelations have happened while trapped in incredibly close quarters. Occasionally with a malfunctioning toilet.

Sharing in the sheer panic of a poop tsunami can teach you a lot about your marriage, and *about yourself.* It's like couple's therapy but with a much higher risk of dysentery. Because, see, love isn't just about cleaning up other's people shit. It's about finding someone who can help *you deal with yours.*

Don't I sound positively authoritative? Like Dr. Phil, only more crap-obsessed? That's the problem with having a blog: people start getting the mistaken impression that you are somehow an authority on what you've chosen to write about. That you actually have a *clue*. At some point, readers may even start soliciting you for advice. This is incredibly dangerous for everyone involved. If enough people start believing that you know what you are talking about, you might start believing it, too.

I do not wield this power wisely.

Once, while Rand and I were walking in downtown Seattle, a middle-aged couple pulled over and asked us where they could find a liquor store. Rand began to tell them that there weren't any liquor stores nearby, which was true, because he has this nasty habit of letting facts get in the way of his helping people.

That's never been a problem of mine. I chimed in that there was a liquor store just down and over a few blocks. The couple listened intently as I gave them very specific directions that were entirely incorrect.

They thanked me and drove off, and we continued on our walk, a slight spring now added to my step. I was downright pleased with myself.

"I can't believe I was able to help them," I said, delighted.

"Yeah," Rand said, somewhat skeptically. "I didn't think there was a liquor store down here."

"Of course there is—we went there the other day to grab a soda—Pete's or whatever."

"Pete's?"

"Yeah. The place on the corner, with the big green sign."

"Wait . . . you mean Ralph's?"

"Yeah . . . " I said, the chipperness falling out of my gait. "Ralph's, Pete's—whatever. The point is, it's a liquor store on 3rd." So I'd gotten the name wrong—they'd still find it.

"It's not a liquor store."

"It's not?"

"It's a grocery store."

"Well," I said, all confidence draining out of my voice, "they have liquor, too."

"No, they don't."

"Oh."

"You told them it was on 3rd?"

"Yeah."

"It's not on 3rd. Baby, where did you send them?"

According to Google Maps, my directions could have landed them either at the Jewish Community Center or a Moroccan restaurant, and to this day, I comfort myself with the thought that probably, maybe at least one of those establishments sold booze.

"If you knew my directions were wrong, why didn't you stop me?" I asked.

"Because you sounded so . . . so *confident.*"

I have no idea what became of that couple. Odds are, they probably gave up, headed home with some takeout Moroccan, and had a nice, quiet, disappointingly sober evening. But some small part of me is convinced that they are circling those blocks down which I sent them, doomed to spend an eternity yelling to each other, "It must be here. She said it was here. And she sounded so *confident.*"

The point is, asking me for travel advice is a terrible idea, and it will ruin your marriage, if not your life. And yet I still get people emailing me, wondering which hotel they should pick for their visit to Bulgaria (short answer: don't go to Bulgaria).

They email me about other things, too, like love and marriage. But here is where things differ: even though the basic rules of properly interacting with strangers utterly elude me, and I occasionally lead innocent couples on a road to nowhere, I am pretty sure I've managed to figure out this whole happily-ever-after stuff.

I figure even a stopped clock is right twice a day, so why can't this stopped clock have a successful relationship?

What time is it?

IT IS BLISS O'CLOCK, YOU FOOLS.

Whenever I am asked about it, I always give the same response: if you want to be absurdly happy, marry someone you love whom you can spend time with. But most importantly, marry someone who can help you deal with your shit.

In the spring of 2011, a little more than two years after I'd started my blog, we found ourselves in New York City once again, and I was about to become acutely aware of how true my advice was and of how well my dear husband helped me deal with mine. Because there, in a tiny room in an environmentally conscious hotel on 47th Street, a series of events transpired that I could not have handled alone. We would, when searching for the specific words to describe the gravitas of the situation, come to describe it as A-pooh-calypse.

A-pooh-calypse began innocuously enough, as all disasters do.

We checked into our room and found that our green, LEED-certified accommodations looked more or less like any other hotel room, except that there were fliers all over the place telling you precisely how many owls and leatherback turtles had been spared in the creation of the hotel.

In the bathroom, I found a bar of soap that had no middle—it was shaped like a rectangular doughnut. The packaging briefly mentioned that the unique shape was good for the environment and that the creation of it required 40 percent fewer resources than a regular bar of soap. It instantly broke into several pieces the first time I tried washing my hands, because a doughnut has less structural integrity than a bar.

I mashed the soap fragments together into a lumpy abomination, which I noted was roughly 40 percent smaller than a regular bar of soap.

"What the hell happened?" Rand asked when he saw it, and I told him that every time he used a regular bar of soap, a baby seal died.

Not to be left out, the adjacent toilet featured a water-saving, low-flow design. Rather than flush your waste away like its environmentally hostile counterparts, a low-flow toilet dribbles a bit of water into the bowl and slowly swishes things around. You get to watch your turds twirl about like putrid little synchronized swimmers, and in seeing this, you know that you've made the world a better place.

I did not realize this was the case with our toilet when I performed the ladylike act of graciously emptying my bowels into it. Presuming that it worked like virtually every other toilet in the developed world, I lowered the lid, flushed, and went out to explore the city with my beloved.

Now, in order for you to fully understand the significance of this story and the depth of my husband's love and tolerance, I need to take a moment to describe my bowels and the contents therein. (May god have mercy on us all.)

The general consensus is that any solid waste coming from a woman, and a woman under five feet three at that, should be in the form of tiny and inoffensive pellets, like what you might find at the bottom of a rabbit hutch.

In what may be the understatement of the year, and perhaps my lifetime, let me simply say: Nope.

The point is, those of us who are smallest in stature are occasionally giants when it comes to pooping. Plato said that, I think. But let's make it official:

> Even the smallest in stature can be pooping giants.
> —Plato

* * *

WHEN RAND AND I RETURNED to our hotel room a few hours later, we noticed it smelled more like feces than hotel rooms usually do, and Rand, in an effort to locate the origin of the offense, traced it to the bathroom.

"Dear god, baby," he said. "Why didn't you flush?"

I explained that I had, and I squeezed into the closet-sized bathroom with him only to find that our low-flow toilet had ignored my attempt to dispose of my filth. The bowl was now filled with putrid water, murky and horrific after three hours of stewing.

"Shit," I said, stating the obvious.

I tried flushing again and heard the sickening sound of a tank filling, and nothing else. The toilet had clogged, its delicate, baby seal–friendly plumbing unable to deal with any waste that wasn't reconstituted kale.

I called maintenance.

A few minutes later there was a knock at our door, and I opened it to find a bright-eyed young man in coveralls, holding a plunger. His nametag read "Eduardo."

I think most of us reach that pivotal point in adulthood at which we have the chance to step up and deal with our own shit, or have someone else do it. And I am going to tell you right now that you should absolutely have someone else do it and then tip them an absurd amount, apologize profusely, and hope you never see them again.

That is what I should have done.

Instead, I took the plunger from Eduardo with a quick thank you, and, in a shockingly misplaced display of confidence, headed to the bathroom.

"Baby," Rand said, following me at a distance, "are you sure you've got it?"

I nodded, but still he remained close, just outside the splash radius, his face a mask of utter disgust as I lowered the plunger into the murk with the caution of one defusing a bomb.

"Careful," Rand said, his voice barely a whisper.

"I know, I know."

Delicately, so as not to splash, I pressed the plunger down a few times, reducing whatever solids remained in the bowl into the unholiest of soups.

"I think that's enough," Rand said.

I wasn't quite as convinced, but I so wanted him to be right that I took the plunger out, gave it a gentle shake, and laid it on a piece of newspaper I'd had the foresight to lay down in the corner.

And then I flushed the toilet.

If you are eating lunch right now, I suggest you put this book down. If your life has been relatively stress- and trauma-free until this point, feel free to skip to the end of the chapter. But if you have lived through war, or are a surgeon in the trauma ward of a major hospital, or have a toddler, then read on. You have seen these horrors before.

Water began to flow into the bowl, and the putrescent tide began to rise. I watched, unbelieving, as the water climbed higher and higher toward the lip of the bowl. I kept thinking it would stop and the panic that was rising at the same rate inside my chest would dissipate as well.

But it did not.

I lived a lifetime in those brief seconds.

I contemplated making a break for it. I imagined turning to Rand and screaming, "RUN!" We'd tear out of our hotel room and down the stairs, as the toilet overflowed and sent a brown wave crashing after us.

We'd reach the street and continue to race through Midtown New York, into the lights and noise of the human pinball machine that is Times Square. We'd try to blend in, to erase the panic and horror from our faces. We'd change our names and start a new life, never speaking of that hotel and the things we'd seen inside.

What better place to start over than New York City? If we could make it there, we could make it anywhere, provided there were industrial-strength toilets.

* * *

ALAS, THIS WASN'T EVEN THE first time I'd been in this kind of situation. In December 2001, when Rand and I had only been dating a few weeks, I found myself alone in his apartment. I was still in school; he'd just dropped out and was working full-time.

Rand had already left for the day, leaning in close to my ear and whispering that I should sleep in before kissing me goodbye. I curled up in his fluffy comforter and scooted over into the warm spot he'd left on the bed.

I stared at the ceiling and smiled. I liked him. I liked him in spite of myself and that deep-seated desire I had to be miserable and alone. I liked him even though I didn't want to. I finally got out of the warm cocoon of bed to use the bathroom, relieved that he was not around. In those days, there was still mystery left.

And then I flushed.

The water did not go down. Instead, it began to rise, a vile broth inching higher and higher toward the lip of the bowl.

I panicked. If the toilet began to overflow, I reasoned that I could just run. Grab my pants and shoes from the floor of his room and just leave. I wouldn't call him again.

Rand would wonder, of course, what had happened. He might even start to worry. But then he'd think of the carnage in the bathroom and know that it was all for the best.

But I didn't want it to end like that.

"Stop," I pleaded desperately of the toilet bowl. "Please, just stop."

Miraculously, the septic gods heard my prayer, and the water stopped rising. With a few desperate thrusts of the plunger, the clog was dispatched. The toilet flushed.

He never knew about the carnage I could create until we moved in together. And by then it was too late. We'd already combined our CD collections, and in the early 2000s there was no greater sign of commitment.

And now there he was, in a cramped hotel room with me in New York City, staring at the contents of the bowl with thinly veiled horror. It soon became clear that unlike the bathroom in

Rand's apartment all those years ago, this toilet had no automatic shut-off. It was going to overflow.

"Trashcan," I said to Rand, with uncharacteristic calmness. He needed no other explanation. In one smooth, fluid motion, he grabbed it (it was, miraculously, not wicker or made from repurposed magazines, but composed of sturdy, dolphin-choking plastic), dumped the contents on the floor of the bathroom, and handed it to me.

And then, much as my ancestors did, I began to bail the water out of the toilet and into the shower.

As I did so, Rand had maneuvered around me and taken the lid off the top of the tank. He'd discovered the source of the problem: the chain had caught on some small apparatus that had been placed inside the tank to save water. The toilet would have filled indefinitely.

He delicately unhooked the chain and was able to stop the rising toilet water, but not before I'd bailed several trashcans full into the shower. As quickly as it had begun, it was over.

We stared blankly at each other, the last two survivors at the end of a horror movie. We'd done it.

Of course, the toilet was still clogged, and there were now turds clogging the shower drain, but honestly, that could be said of most hotels in Midtown, right?

No? Okay, fine.

I asked Rand to bring me some cleaning supplies.

"From the hotel?" he asked.

I shook my head. If the soap was any indication, the housekeeping staff probably had to clean the bathrooms with lavender oil and crystals.

"I need bleach," I said.

I should note: Rand tends to get sick a lot on the road. In addition to the pain in his leg and back that constantly bugs him, he interacts with so many people at meetings and conferences that he often ends up with a miserable cold. At that moment, he was suffering from both. And so, in the middle of the night, my poor husband, who was already feeling dizzy and feverish and unsteady before any of this had happened, rushed into the madness of Times Square to locate cleaning supplies.

This left me to tend to the postdiluvian bathroom, with the still-clogged toilet. I decided that I was going to really plunge the hell out of the thing.

And it is at this point in the story that my logic ran out. (I am my mother's daughter, after all.)

Since I didn't want to worry about splashes, I figured I should remove all my clothes, save for a pair of black underwear (because I reasoned that plunging a toilet while totally naked would be weird). And since I didn't want to get my hair dirty, I put on a shower cap.

And then, for reasons that still escape me, I decided to put my shoes back on.

I plunged. And I plunged. I splashed water with abandon, which landed pretty much everywhere, including onto the shoes that I was inexplicably wearing.

That was the scene that Rand returned to, and to his credit, he said nothing. That's one of the great things about marriage. At some point, your beloved will inevitably find you mostly naked, shower-capped, and furiously plunging away, and they'll just hand you a bag of cleaning supplies without comment.

I realized that, in using those products, I'd officially destroyed the hotel's eco-friendly status, but it could be argued that that had happened hours before when this entire debacle began. Besides, I was sure I'd be hard-pressed to find someone who felt that bleach wasn't required.

And so I cleaned. I polished the floor, where the water had splashed, I cleaned the toilet seat, and then I tackled the shower.

I sprayed the cleanser throughout, scrubbed with paper towels, every action a wasteful crime against the planet. I turned the water in the shower as hot as it would go, and when I was through, I did it all again. And then I did it a third time, just for good measure.

When I was done, the bathroom sparkled.

And then I finally stepped into the shower myself, scrubbing my skin with the nub of misshapen soap, until my body squeaked with cleanliness.

I emerged from the bathroom, which smelled of chlorine and antiseptic, to find Rand curled up on the bed, half-asleep. I lay down next to him.

"Baby," I whispered, "it's done."

I felt like an assassin, having cleaned up after that one final job.

Rand's eyes fluttered open. He looked at me for a long time before he spoke.

"Sweetie?" he asked.

"Yeah?"

"What the fuck."

"Yeah," I said. "Yeah."

And then we went to sleep.

The preceding story should immediately disqualify me from dispelling advice on most topics, and possibly from being allowed to rent a hotel room in the Tri-State area ever again. I can barely dispose of waste in a device *whose sole purpose is to do just that.* Do not ask me where to stay in New York City. I have no answers to that riddle, which has plagued humanity for so long.

Instead, make your queries about something I can actually answer: feces.

No, wait, no. That's wrong. Relationships. Ask me about those. Because if you want to know the key to making one work, the solution really is simple. You just need to find someone who will help you deal with your shit.

8

LISTEN TO YOUR HEART, EVEN IF IT TELLS YOU TO STEAL THINGS

OTHERS, WHEN DESCRIBING the alchemy of a happy life, do not speak of poop. They likely do not speak of urine or revenge, either. I don't do things properly. I'm trying to accept that.

I've always had trouble reckoning with my own mistakes, which is unfortunate, given how prone I am to making them.

For examples, please see Chapter 1, Chapter 2, Chapters 4–7, that time I pierced my belly button, that time I thought Scotland was an island, that time I ate a salad I bought in an airport, that time I went on the Gravitron, every haircut I had between 1988 and 2004, those two years I spent doing hot yoga. The time I purchased those glorious black ankle boots, wore them exactly once so as to render them unreturnable, and then realized they were the wrong size. That time *I* put the wrong soap in the dishwasher and flooded the kitchen with suds (I lied before when I said it was Rand). The fact that I never once told that boy who lived next door to me in the dorms sophomore year that I thought he was wonderful. The fact that it took me so long to realize that Rand was.

Some of these mistakes haunt me. On sleepless nights, plagued by jet lag, I stare up at the ceiling of my hotel room and replay scenes from my past. I cringe. This is a thoroughly unproductive exercise, and I am the reigning world champion.

I think about the day I screwed up the time of a reservation for a fancy dinner we'd already paid for in Edinburgh. We were supposed to go with our preternaturally laid-back friends Wil and Nora, and I'd spent so much time fretting about the dress code that I got us there three hours late (in my defense, who eats dinner at 4:45?).

Nora shrugged, Wil insisted he wasn't even hungry, and Rand tried to comfort me as I stood, shockingly overdressed with absolutely no place to go, and struggled not to panic.

All I've ever wanted in life is to feel that I knew what the hell I was doing. That I'm in control. And travel offers the exact opposite of that experience. Every trip is just an opportunity to screw up on a grand scale. Every trip is an exercise in handing the reigns over to someone else, or letting them go altogether.

I think, if I were a better person, I'd be more accepting of that fact. I'd be more forgiving of myself and others. I'd have some perspective on the matter and wouldn't respond to my errors the way I do—which is, generally speaking, with either a panicked freak-out, some weird act of passive-aggressive revenge at whatever other culpable parties I can identify, or both.

And I'm trying to come to terms with that, too. Sometimes, you just need to accept that you aren't perfect—that you screw up, that you can be petty, that you can be vengeful and small, ideally in a country where your fingerprints aren't on record.

It's something I'm still working on. But I'd like to think that I'm making progress.

It was the fall of 2011, just a few short months after the flood of putrescence we narrowly avoided in New York. Rand had a conference in Barcelona that October, and I, still thoroughly unqualified for most fields of employment and content to let my sole houseplant die, went along with him. (RIP, dear peace lily. You never knew the tranquility promised by your name.)

Two of his coworkers—Kenny and Joanna—were with us, and since I liked them and didn't want word to get out that Rand was, in actuality, married to a hastily shorn ape in skinny jeans, I was determined to be on my best behavior. I wanted to show them I knew what the hell I was doing.

I didn't actually succeed, mind you, but I tried, and that's what's important.

Of the four of us, I was the most proficient in Spanish. This meant that I had once studied it in high school and, despite forgetting most of it thanks to recreational drug use in college, felt fairly confident that I could order us dinner without accidentally propositioning the waiter for sex.

Most of the time, though, I got stressed when speaking with locals and resorted to one of two phrases:

"Dónde está el baño?" ("Where is the bathroom?")
This phrase is not only useful but gives you an
opportunity to easily leave whatever conversation

you've gotten yourself into. The only downside, you'll soon realize, is that you won't be able to understand the directions given to you in reply. You will then have to pretend that you weren't the one who peed in the broom closet.

"Creo que esto fue un error." ("I think this was a mistake.") Inexplicably, this phrase (found in the "Nightlife" section of my phrasebook, under the heading "Cooling Down") remained stuck in my head for much of the trip. I couldn't ask for a doctor in case of an emergency, but I was totally ready to express regret should I happen to have a one-night stand with a Spaniard.

Fortunately, the mechanics of this particular trip meant that I needed to use very little of my abysmal Spanish. Instead, we took a bus tour and spent the better part of the day gawking at the incredible architecture in the city.

That's one of the best things about Barcelona: you'll head down an inconspicuous tree-lined street, and the buildings will all be quite formal and neoclassical until—BOOM—you run into an apartment building designed by Antoni Gaudí that looks like a very elaborate seascape with a giant iguana sleeping on top. Or you'll find yourself face-to-face with an enormous sculpture by the artist Joan Miró that resembles a half-digested chew toy.

And we tourists will stand and marvel and take photos while the Spanish just shrug it off as if it isn't a big deal and carry on with their day, heading into office buildings that resemble two giant mating mollusks.

I suppose it's a cultural thing. Perhaps eating dinner at midnight and taking a nap in the middle of the workday gives you a high tolerance for weird, and I think we can all learn a valuable lesson from that.

After a day touring the city, we found ourselves near the waterfront and—realizing we were all tired and peckish (a potential disaster for any group touring a city, because it is during those times of exhaustion and low blood sugar that things are said that cannot be unsaid and relationships end)—we popped into the nearest café we could find.

It, like virtually every other restaurant, bar, or gas station in Spain, served tapas. The Spanish invented these small dishes—usually tiny snacks speared on a toothpick—presumably in order to make amends to humanity for the Inquisition.

"Sorry we murdered and tortured everyone in the name of Christ. Here, try this ham. It's made from a pig that spent its life drinking port wine while being read the works of Cervantes."

The café was clean and had a view of the Mediterranean—two factors that caused us all to ignore the rather alarming fact that it had absolutely zero customers. Also, the proprietor may have cackled with glee when he saw that we were all Americans, though I may have imagined that.

So, against my better judgment (which, I've come to believe, may not exist at all) we sat down and looked at the menu. The prices weren't unreasonable, and so we ordered a few dishes.

"Pan con tomate?" the waiter suggested.

"Si, si!" someone shouted.

"Sangria?" the waiter offered again.

"Si, si!"

It was only after we ordered that I realized neither of these items appeared on the menu. I nervously pointed this out to

Rand. My dining experiences in Europe had taught me that whenever the staff suggested something off-menu, it's best to just hand them your entire wallet and whatever jewelry you might be wearing, because whatever you just ordered is going to cost an absolute fortune. I usually like to throw my pants in, too, just for good measure, at which point Rand tells me I'm being melodramatic and to stop shedding my clothes in public.

In this instance, though, we were with his coworkers, so I kept my pants on and instead just voiced my worries quietly and nervously to my husband.

"It will be fine," Rand told me. Which is also what people probably said when Franco rose to power.

Our waiter returned a short while later with a plate of cured ham, some blistered padron peppers sprinkled with sea salt, and massive goblets filled with red wine and fruit. After a few tentative sips, I'd decided that he was my best friend, even if he was buying a boat at our expense.

And then the pan con tomate arrived.

Now, my memory is a bit hazy—I'm not much of a drinker and I'd already had two tablespoons of sangria—but I seem to remember that the pile of doughy slices was roughly the size of a Volkswagen, sloshed with what appeared to be ketchup, and looking thoroughly unappetizing.

The waiter scurried back into the kitchen before we had time to stop him or to communicate, in broken Spanish, that he'd given us enough bread to kill an elephant with celiac disease.

And then I realized: we were about to be charged an exorbitant amount for that pile of bread. And I had let it happen.

Now, usually, usually, when you order pan con tomate in Spain, you will find that it is something that far transcends the sum of its parts, not unlike a 90s-era boy band. You find yourself biting into a crusty piece of fresh bread, onto which the inside of a ripe, juicy tomato has been vigorously rubbed. A drizzle of fruity olive oil and a sprinkle of salt and freshly ground pepper go over the top, and it tastes not unlike a cold piece of rustic pizza.

My point is that done properly it is very, very good.

I took a tentative bite of one slice, realizing that sometimes looks can be deceiving. In this instance, they were not.

"This is awful," I said, swallowing a doughy lump. "And I bet they're going to charge us a fortune for it."

"It's fine," Rand said.

"It is *not* fine," I snapped, loudly enough for the others to hear. I'd screwed up again.

He stared at me, pleading, while Joanna and Kenny stayed silent, watching the drama unfold while nibbling on tapas.

"Baby, please," he said. "Don't get mad about this. It's really not a big deal."

"But they're going to overcharge us—" I began, and that's when Rand pulled out the heavy artillery.

"So what? I'd gladly pay three times whatever the bill is, if it meant that you weren't upset."

See how terrible he is? He's constantly trying to deprive me of my own rage, even if that rage is directed at myself. And he was right. It was a plate of *bread*. There are bigger battles to be fought, ones far more important than those waged over carbohydrates.

But I couldn't let it go. It was a minor thing, but this only frustrated me more because I hadn't been able to prevent it. I'd figured the whole point of me tagging along to Spain was to make sure that things went smoothly and no one was over-charged, which I'd somehow hoped to manage with three years of high school Spanish and a phrasebook that was largely dedicated to sexual intercourse. Otherwise, what the hell was I doing on this trip? Or, for that matter, with my life? And what was I thinking when I shaved my head but inexplicably left my bangs long during sophomore year of college?

I mean, I give Rick Steves a hard time for wandering around the planet dressed like a substitute math teacher, but it's not like he would have let this happen, right? WHAT SORT OF CRAPPY TRAVEL WRITER ALLOWS HERSELF TO GET RIPPED OFF OVER STALE BREAD?

I felt my anxiety rise, blowing the situation well out of proportion. Unemployed Geraldine had *one* job, and she had failed at it. I should have stayed at home. I made a lot fewer mistakes when I never left the house.

I exhaled heavily and tried to mentally prepare myself for the bill.

"Even if it it's five euros, I will be calm," I thought.

When the bill arrived Rand lunged for it, but I managed to sneak a glance.

Every item we'd ordered that hadn't been listed on the menu was 2–3 times the price we'd seen elsewhere. And then I saw the last line.

Pan con tomate x 4 . . . 12 euros.

Now, I'm not sure if you are familiar with exchange rates, and granted, they fluctuate somewhat, but at any given time in Europe, you can be confident that the exchange rate with the dollar hovers between "Oh, dear god" and "I HAVE TO MORTGAGE MY UTERUS."

Two drinks and three small plates of tapas, including the bread, came to nearly $100.

In a span of just under two seconds, I lost whatever semblance of composure I had and began sputtering like a broken coffee maker.

"Baby," Rand pleaded, "just this once, can you please let it go?"

I exhaled heavily. Could I? Maybe just this once? Did the Count of Monte Cristo let things go? Did Don Corleone let things go? Did Uma Thurman's character from *Kill Bill* let things go? No. They killed everyone. Which, okay, granted, doesn't really seem like a responsible course of action, but it gave them closure. And then they found peace, something that my husband expected me to somehow attain by *letting it go.*

But how do you explain to someone that your sense of self-worth is now tethered to your dinner bill?

"*Fine.* I'll let it go."

But I didn't say that. Instead, I stood up and walked directly over to our waiter.

This would have, I suppose, been a perfectly good time to have used one of the two panicked Spanish phrases I had in my repertoire, but rather than wave the check in his face while screaming "CREO QUE ESTO FUE UN ERROR!" I simply inquired where the bathroom was.

I had no idea what he said in reply, but judging by his hand gestures, it was downstairs.

"IT'S FINE," I shouted to Rand as I headed down the steps. "I JUST NEED TO PEE."

I should tell you that I am not proud of what happened next, but I'd be lying, because I sort of am.

I was hovering some distance above the toilet seat (which is what I do whenever using a public bathroom), thinking about the twelve damn euros. And, I realized a way that I'd be able to let go of my anger. Slowly, I began to sway side to side, like some sort of strange, urine-streaming pendulum.

By the time I was done, I had sufficiently saturated the bathroom. I surveyed the scene proudly and walked out without flushing.

I know you're thinking: that whoever had to clean that up didn't deserve any of it, but I'd like to defend myself with the following arguments:

1. I was drunk on sangria.
2. Peeing all over the place made me feel a lot better.
3. I didn't kill anyone.
4. I screw up a lot (see the entire rest of this book).

When you consider that, I think my actions become morally justifiable. Sometimes, it seems, the only way to reckon with your own mistakes is to make even more of them.

I walked upstairs and found everyone seated at the table, waiting for me.

"Where's the bathroom?" Joanna asked.

"You don't want to use it," I said.

"It's *that* bad?"

"Yes." (This was now true.)

I looked around—Rand had paid the bill, and the waiter had retreated to the back of the café. We were all alone.

I grabbed a napkin dispenser and shoved it into my bag.

"What the hell are you doing?" Rand asked.

"They charged us twelve euros for bread, so I'm taking this."

"Don't take the napkin dispenser," Kenny said, shaking his head.

I looked at him, and at the dispenser that was sticking halfway out of my purse. I thought of how desperately I needed to regain control of the situation. How badly I wanted to prove to myself—and everyone else—that I knew what I was doing. Sheepishly, I removed it and placed it back on the table.

"If anything," he said, picking up one of the sangria goblets, "you should take this."

Joanna, standing nearby, was nodding her agreement.

"Do it," she said. "Hurry."

They helped me slip the glass into my bag while Rand stared blankly at the three of us, trying to understand when, exactly, he had lost control of the situation.

"Should I take a napkin dispenser, too?" I asked.

"WE'RE LEAVING," Rand said, quickly pushing us out before I could abscond with anything else in the name of justice.

We walked into the night, a tiny bit of light still hovering over the horizon, turning the sky violet.

Still buzzing with energy from the thrill of my small heist, I pulled the goblet from my bag and held it up proudly.

"I can't believe you," Rand said, shaking his head. He was partly in shadow, but I could see he was smiling.

"I had to do it. It was the only way I could get over it. They charged us twelve euros for bread, so I had to steal their glass and pee all over their bathroom."

"Wait, what?"

"I peed all over the toilet seat. And maybe a little on the floor. I had to. So I could let it go, like you told me to."

"You *peed all over their bathroom?*"

"Yes, and now we're even, so I've let it go."

"That is not at all what I meant."

Oh. Huh.

Later, Kenny would proudly tell everyone in the office about my drunken misdeeds while Rand repeatedly reminded everyone that my actions were not representative of the company or its executive team. He maintains to this day that conflicts should not be resolved via theft and/or urination.

And he's right, of course. I screwed up big time on this one. I'm tempted to fixate on it, as I always do. But that never gets me anywhere.

Instead, I try to focus on one of the few things I've done right—I've surrounded myself with people in life who are far more forgiving of me than I am of myself. They remain through the mistakes, through the wrong turns and the missed reservations and the overpriced bread, through the anxiety that weaves through all of it, through the brief but powerful bouts of revenge that I enact in order to make myself feel better. I think of the time I botched dinner in Edinburgh, Wil stood in the middle of the street and started inexplicably dancing.

"Chill out, G," he said, entirely unconcerned.

I am reminded that my mistakes don't mean I'm a failure as a human. They just mean I'm human.

And more constant than all these unwavering people is Rand. He tells me that it will be okay. He reminds me that there are bigger battles to fight. That you can't control everything, and if you try, you'll drive yourself mad and have to saturate a lot of things with pee. And I try to listen, again and again, repeating what he says to me whenever I feel that I've committed some

unforgivable sin. Whenever I've absconded with some item because I felt slighted or peed all over something in the name of
justice.

"Geraldine, just let it go."

On the streets of Barcelona, I tried to do just that. We
passed a garbage can, and I stared at the goblet for a moment
before dropping it inside. In the end, I really did let it go.

9

HOME IS WHERE
YOUR MRI IS

IN THE THREE YEARS SINCE I had started my blog, we spent large chunks of time on the road. But despite health code violations in New York hotels, or pilgrimages across London to find ancient clocks, or the crimes undertaken on the shores of the Mediterranean, Seattle was always home. We left for a few weeks but invariably returned to the same place. It was always just as we left it—the overcast skies, the squeaky spot on the stairs, the potato that I refused to throw out—despite Rand's pleas—because I wanted to see if it would grow into a tree (current status: not yet, but I have faith).

Hometowns tend to get a bad rap. I suspect it's because most of our lives happens there. And so the good and the bad, the highs and the lows, all get attributed to a town that's not really to blame. It's just that you happened to live there when things started to go awry. The unpaid bills, the parking tickets, the tearful break-ups, and that driver who inexplicably gave you the middle finger after he cut you off all become symptoms of your own geography.

You become so bogged down with the difficulties of the everyday that you never step back and see it for what it is. Which is a shame, especially if you live in the most beautiful place in the world. And the subjectivity of that statement means that so, so many of us do.

Seattle was where I was born. Under a gray, cloudy sky, I learned to walk and read and ride a two-wheeled bike and drive a car. I had my senior prom at the Seattle Aquarium and ate burgers from Dick's Drive-In late on college nights when I was hungry and my metabolism could handle such abuse. I kissed boys in the shadow of the Space Needle and borrowed their flannel shirts when the night grew cold. I once saw Dave Matthews at the QFC in Wallingford and the guitarist from Soundgarden walking by the Whole Foods on Roosevelt.

This was where I met Rand and where he first kissed me, a move that took me by such surprise that I asked him if he had just done it.

"Nope," he lied, before leaning in to do it again.

I fell in love in this city and with this city. And in June 2012, after three years spent traveling with Rand and writing about our adventures on the road, it was here that I found out I had a brain tumor.

I'm probably breaking all sorts of rules by telling you about it up front. I'm pretty sure the laws of memoirs demand that I reveal the news to you slowly or provide some sort of buildup, or foreshadowing, or something. But that's never how bad news is delivered in real life. It just happens, abruptly and without warning, on warm spring days when we're still in our pajamas. So that's how I'm telling you.

I'd been having headaches for the better part of a decade, but over the last few years they'd gotten steadily worse. By the time I was finally laid off from my job, I felt some measure of relief. The headaches had become a daily occurrence, and working at my desk or simply checking my email had become excruciating.

I was able to step back from my computer and bask in my unemployment for a while; the headaches subsided. But in the months since, they'd returned and gotten steadily worse. By the spring of 2012, they'd gotten so bad that I could barely function. Even something as simple as folding laundry was difficult. Writing the blog was excruciating.

I hail from a long, nervous line of hypochondriacs. My mother had spent the last three decades explaining to me why everyone and everything were out to get me. So in yet another unconscious act of defiance, I had been dismissing the daily pain in my skull as nothing.

"Everyone gets headaches," I told Rand, when he expressed worry.

"Not every day, they don't."

But I had long ago decided that people complained about headaches when they had no bigger struggle to worry about. This was no big deal. Then came the road trip we took down to Portland, Oregon, for a weekend. I don't remember much of it, except for the journey home. I was hit with a headache so severe that I couldn't drive.

"You need to talk to your doctor," Rand said, as I slumped in the passenger seat.

I would have nodded, defeated, but I was unable to move my head or neck, so I just mumbled assent while I tried to find a comfortable position for the three-hour ride home. There wasn't one. It hurt to lie down. It hurt to sleep.

The next week, when I went to see my doctor, she suggested an MRI.

"I highly doubt we'll find anything," she said, "but I'd like to do it anyway. For peace of mind."

She gave me a list of imaging centers around the city, and the one with the earliest available appointment was in Ballard.

Ballard, a little neighborhood in northwestern Seattle, is where I lived when I was very young. My earliest memories of Seattle—and my earliest memories, period—take place there. Before the music and tech scenes emerged to put us on the map, before there were traffic jams and gastropubs and million-dollar condos, there was a Denny's where my mother would order me popcorn shrimp and a convenience store where my uncle would buy me windup toys that would instantly break.

Few vestiges remain of the Scandinavian fishing village it once was, those having been replaced by trendy restaurants that refuse to take reservations and at least twenty-three places to get a cup of coffee that aren't Starbucks (and five that are). But the occasional bearded hipster will walk by in braids and leather boots, channeling some long-forgotten Norse god, and I'll be reminded of everything it once was.

My technician for my MRI was tall, blond, and altogether far too handsome to put me at ease. He had a hint of a southern accent ("Louisiana," he explained, which was entirely unfair of him. I am happily married). I told him about my headaches, and he repeated my doctor's words of comfort: it was probably nothing.

That made me feel marginally better.

If you've never had an MRI, it is an entirely strange and futuristic experience. The machine operates through a series of magnets, so you have to remove any scrap of metal from your body. I'd taken off my watch and wedding ring, and swapped my jeans for scrubs. I ditched my underwire bra and prayed Mr. Louisiana didn't notice. I pried the jewelry from my ears and nose. (Afterward, I found myself staring at three identical hoops and couldn't for the life of me figure out which went where. Already, I had too many holes in my head.)

You lie down on a sort of dolly that's parallel to the floor and will be loaded, with you on it, into a huge plastic tube.

If you are a claustrophobe like me, I highly recommend that you have a brief talk with the technician to establish an understanding that in the event of a zombie apocalypse or earthquake (I regard both as being equally likely, a result of watching *Night of the Living Dead* at a tender young age), they agree to come get you out of the machine. Failing that, they'll at least scream so you know to climb out yourself instead of just lying there, waiting to be eaten. Or crushed. But let's be reasonable: eaten is way more likely.

I know it seems like I'm trying to make a joke here, but I have had many, many MRIs, and before each I have had that same critical discussion. It's important to be an advocate for your own health.

Zombie emergency protocols firmly in place, you lie down, and someone jams earplugs into your ears. I know that seems like the sort of thing you want to do yourself, but believe me:

you very much want a professional jamming those things in. I realize that all the times I'd ever put in earplugs, I'd done a half-assed job of it, whereas the technicians shove them in so far that they're basically knuckle-deep in your ear canal.

After the earplugs are in, they place a pair of giant headphones over your ears, which is as close as most of us will ever come to knowing the glory felt by those people with the glowing wands that help direct planes at the airport. The headphones are connected to a microphone in the technician's center so they can tell you what's going on and alert you in the event of earthquakes or zombie attacks, as they promised. Miraculously, you will be able to hear them through the earplugs.

Then—it's up to you at this point—you can choose to have a blindfold put over your eyes. I always choose a blindfold, which is rather out of character, but it's nice to know that sometimes you can surprise yourself. Normally, if you're about to be loaded into a strange tube that makes you easy pickings for the undead, I'd understand you wanting to keep your eyes open so you can fight them off. But with brain MRIs, they also lock your head into a plastic case that looks sort of like an old-fashioned birdcage. If you are a claustrophobe, the blindfold comes in handy because you can pretend you are actually lying in a much more spacious place, like a coffin or the trunk of someone's car.

Next, the technician will hand you a small rubber bulb-like device to squeeze if you need to be let out of your plastic prison. I don't know if it actually works, but it serves as a very effective security blanket.

And then you are loaded into the massive tube. You can feel the track moving beneath you and the light (as it comes in through the blindfold) dim. The only thing you need to do is lie perfectly still, which is incredibly easy to do unless someone has told you to lie perfectly still, at which point it is fucking impossible.

Once inside, you can't breathe too deeply, or swallow, or flinch, or wiggle your toes for fear of messing things up. Once the scan starts, so do the noises. An MRI sounds *exactly* like putting a chainsaw into a garbage disposal, or possibly the passionate mating sounds of a fax machine and a semiautomatic rifle. Sometimes the sounds are softer pulses. Sometimes the noises are so loud the entire machine shakes (while you, feebly, try to remain perfectly still).

Forgive me for bragging about this, but that first MRI I had—I rocked the *hell* out of it. I was motionless and serene, my breathing shallow, like at the end of a yoga class but with significantly less farting. It helped that, at the time, I felt perfectly calm. I was just in there to confirm that nothing was wrong.

Roughly a week later, I would learn another valuable lesson about getting MRIs: hysterical crying immediately prior to one is a terrible idea. Snot drips down the back of your throat, and if you try clearing it or swallowing, you move too much and mess up the scans. But that usually only happens after the second or third MRI, and if those are necessary, I feel that tears are understandable.

But during that first scan, I felt completely at peace, an unlikely by-product of my upbringing. I'd spent the first part of my life convinced that everything was trying to kill me, and now that I'd survived the obviously deadly activities of trick or treating and college, I no longer had a reasonable sense of risk or my own mortality.

After the scan was over, I changed back into my clothes and headed back to my car. Because Seattle isn't so great at city planning, and Ballard is no exception, it turns out that one of the best views in the neighborhood is actually from one of upper levels of the Swedish Hospital parking lot.

And as I came across that view, I stopped to look at it. In the coming months, I'd meet my friend Chad, who has brain cancer. One of his most salient pieces of advice was this: "Stop and smell the fucking roses." Take a moment to appreciate how damn beautiful and wonderful the world around you is, and how fantastic it is to be alive. Back then, I didn't know to do things like that. It didn't occur to me. But on that afternoon, for whatever reason, I did.

The clouds were high-altitude and stippled across the sky. The breeze felt warm, and the air smelled like summer was on its way. For the first time that year, I didn't need to put on my coat.

There, in the parking lot, I thought about how nice it was to be home. About how no place in the world felt like this, and how, if I ever had to leave for real, I'd be heartbroken.

I *know*. In hindsight, it sounds positively contrived, like a scene added into a movie to build tension. But as I stood there, all I could think was how wonderful it all was and how lucky I felt. Sometimes, life can be weirdly poetic like that.

Before I left, the dishy Louisianan told me not to worry if I didn't hear from them for a while—it didn't mean anything was wrong. Scans just took a while to read. I'd probably receive a call the following week.

The phone rang the next morning. It was my doctor. The scans had shown a 1-centimeter nodular lesion on my hypothalamus.

I had a brain tumor.

10

IT'S ALWAYS EASIER TO LEAVE FOR A TRIP THAN TO BE LEFT BEHIND

THERE ARE THINGS THAT YOU can imagine yourself saying.

Things like, "Why thank you, yes, I will take a fifth helping of dessert."

or

"I have no idea how Jeff Goldblum's entire collection of boxer shorts ended up in the trunk of my car, Officer."

And then there are things that you hope to say one day, like:

"Oh, you are too kind—but if anyone here is a comedic genius, it's you, Ms. Fey. Or may I call you Tina?"

or

"I am so glad that our all-female Supreme Court declared thong underwear unconstitutional."

And then there's shit that you never imagined saying, but somehow, you end up saying it. I'm guessing every single person who's ever uttered "I'm getting a divorce" or "I think this is raccoon meat" has felt this way. The words leave your mouth, and they don't sound real.

And so it was that in the spring of 2012, I sat at my desk and found myself typing these words:

"I have a brain tumor. I've named it Steve."

The standard reaction to this revelation went something like this:

"What the fuck do you mean, 'You have a brain tumor'?"

Followed quickly by, "Wait, why Steve?"

As for why I named it Steve, . . . well, duh. What else was I going to name it? There is no one to whom I am particularly close who is named Steve. I've never kissed a boy named Steve. I've never uttered the phrase, "Steve, I love you." And Steve is nice and short and easy to add to a long list of unrepeatable words. Behold:

"Fucking goddamn miserable piece-of-shit Steve."

See how well that works? It kind of rolls off the tongue. And considering how many big words I was dealing with at the time, I was inclined to stick to something short and sweet and monosyllabic. Besides, the technical name for Steve is a bunch of words I could barely pronounce. When we first learned of him, some overzealous radiologist thought he might be glioma, which is a word that you should not, under any circumstances, look up, because it is bound to lead to an absolutely miserable few days. Trust me on this.

At first, no one even called it a brain tumor, much less by its given name. Not yet. They were describing it as a "nodular lesion"—a medical term that was virtually meaningless, and therefore far less frightening. Naturally, I took to using it.

"I have a nodular lesion. I need to get it biopsied to make sure it's nothing worrisome."

This was far less scary than the alternative: "I have a brain tumor. I'm going to have brain surgery, and they're going to cut the sucker out to see whether or not it's fucking brain cancer."

But eventually the T-word started to take hold, and both my doctors and I started using it. Over the course of a week, I had a series of appointments with different specialists. They asked about my family history. They made me squeeze their fingers with each of my hands. They checked my balance and my ability to follow a flashlight with my eyes.

Rand was with me for those appointments. Trips had been canceled; meetings had been rescheduled. This was unprecedented. As grateful as I was to have him there, I was freaked out by his presence, too, because it was a clear indication that something was wrong. Rand didn't take days off from work. Ever. But there he was, at every one of my of doctor's visits, asking questions while I stared off at the exam room walls. I didn't quite grasp what was happening. Looking back, I still don't.

It was Dr. Foltz, the neurosurgeon who was reviewing my case, who said, after looking at my MRIs, that the surgery would be routine. There was a slight chance of brain cancer—relatively small but still there. The biggest issue was the location of my tumor—it was in a highly problematic place, and according to my most recent MRI, it was creating blood vessels, which meant it was growing. If doctors hadn't found it now, they would have. Like the photo of me from when I was seven and had a mullet, it would come to light, eventually.

I still had trouble accepting the severity of it.

"Just for my own personal benefit, what are the odds that this was a Lego I shoved up my nose when I was three?" I asked Dr. Foltz.

"It's not. We'd be able to see that pretty clearly on the scan."

I'd just learned another important lesson: neurosurgeons are not usually known for their sense of humor.

"We can take this out for you," he said calmly, in his even, soft tone that I still hear sometimes when I think of him. As though he were a dentist, extracting a bad tooth.

"This shouldn't be a problem."

"Oh, good," Rand said, trying to feign optimism as he squeezed my fingers.

I sat there quietly, unsure of what to say or do.

It would become a trend.

* * *

I WASN'T SURE HOW TO prepare for my surgery. I mean, pragmatically speaking, I knew. Dr. Foltz had given me a print-out with specific instructions for the night before. I had to wash my entire body, in particular my scalp and hair, with a special antibacterial soap that was runny and pink and left every part of me dry and brittle.

I had to change my pillowcases and sheets that night and on a nightly basis after I got home.

To make sure that my stomach was empty before I went in, I couldn't consume anything after 9 p.m. (not even water). I had to remove all my jewelry and couldn't wear any substances on my body—not lotion or deodorant or perfume.

All that was fairly easy—a checklist of items that I could cross off one by one. It was everything else—everything that would happen between learning I needed brain surgery and actually getting it—that I was unsure about.

I needed to tell people. But I didn't know how. Rand would soon prove to have an easier time than I did with the task, and before I'd even mentioned it to my family, or any of our friends, he called a company-wide meeting and told all his coworkers that I had a brain tumor.

The only hitch was that he'd neglected to tell *me* about the meeting. I found myself receiving condolence emails from people I barely knew, about what I thought was a private matter.

I was livid. I remember being in the kitchen when I found out what had happened.

"You told everyone you work with? And you didn't think to check with me first? My *mom* doesn't even know."

Rand stared at the ground.

"I'm sorry," he said softly.

I wanted to be angry—but I couldn't be. I couldn't add that on to the pile of everything else Rand felt. It was becoming apparent that this was harder on him than on me.

It was the same when one of us went on a solo trip—whoever stayed behind always felt it more acutely. Dinner alone at home is worse than dinner alone in a new place. At home, you can't escape the fact that something is missing; the house is full of reminders in a way that strange cities aren't. And that's what Rand was terrified of. Being left behind. Alone, surrounded by souvenirs of us.

Besides, I didn't really have the bandwidth to be angry, anyway. I felt that the tumor was taking up valuable real estate in my head. There was only so much room left, and the other emotions—worry, mostly—had squeezed into the space where anger used to fit.

I hugged him. It's something we tend to do on those rare occasions we're upset with each other. Sometimes we hug. Sometimes we hold hands. It's difficult to be angry at someone when you are in the process of actively cuddling them. Toddlers, I think, know this instinctively.

"I fucked up," he said.

"It's okay," I said, as he pressed his face into the curve of my neck and shoulder and shook his head. And then curiosity got the better of me.

"How did they react?" I asked.

"They were all pretty shocked," he said, his voice still quiet, his lips muffled by my neck. "Ruth cried."

"Aww. I love Ruth."

I thought of her, with her soft blonde hair and wire-rimmed glasses. She had a countenance of apple-cheeked sweetness belying a steely sense of resolve and a tendency to tell people to fuck off without hesitation. I had reduced one of the toughest people I knew to tears.

I wrapped my arms around Rand's neck, his face still buried against me. I felt his tears against the collar of my shirt.

Make that two.

✳ ✳ ✳

RAND HAD INADVERTENTLY GOTTEN the ball moving. Many of our friends worked with him; they now knew, as did their spouses. He'd created a strange line of demarcation between who was looped in and who wasn't.

I needed to tell people what was going on. I didn't want someone to hear it from a third party or think I'd hidden it from them for some reason.

I started by making a few phone calls. I should have told my mother in person—a right she had earned. When you help make something, you are entitled to a face-to-face visit when it goes in for repairs. But it was far easier to downplay the situation over the phone.

"The doctor found a small growth," I said, once again avoiding the T-word, "and they're going to biopsy it. There's a teensy chance it might be cancer."

"Where is it?" Mom asked. "On your breast?"

"Um . . . no." I took a breath. "It's on my brain."

"Your *brain*?" Mom repeated it as if she had heard me incorrectly.

"It's just a little brain tumor," I said. *Happens every day, Mom. Hell, you've probably got five of them right now—*

No. That's not the right approach.

I called my aunt and started with the same spiel. Small growth. Small chance of cancer.

"Where is it?" she asked. "On your breast?"

God, NO. What is it with you and my mom and breasts?

"On my brain."

"Your *brain*?" Lather. Rinse. Repeat. Use the runny pink soap every time.

Overall, though, my mom and aunt handled it pretty well. Then I called my brother Edward, who promptly freaked out.

"It's not a big deal," I said.

"WELL IT SURE SOUNDS LIKE A FUCKING BIG DEAL."

There was something inexplicably touching about him yelling at me. Screaming, as a friend of his recently noted, is Edward's love language. He only shouts when he cares. Or when he's mad at the Internet.

But the vast majority of people in my life found out through the blog. It seemed like the easiest way to convey information without breaking into one of those reckless cries in which snot drips down from your nostrils and you don't even really care. I wrote:

> *The good news: the neurosurgeons say there's an 80% chance Steve's benign. If he's not benign, odds are he's still very easily treatable.*
>
> *And then there's the very small chance that he's a more aggressive kind of brain cancer (on the plus side, he's tiny. I think we can deal with tiny and aggressive. Hell, I am tiny and aggressive).*
>
> *Unfortunately, there's no way to definitively figure out what Steve is without a biopsy—which wouldn't be such a big deal except for the fact that Steve's clinging to my hypothalamus like a bride-to-be clutching a Vera Wang gown at Filene's Basement.*
>
> *So they're going to drill a hole in my head, poke some tools through my non-dominant frontal lobe, and pull off a piece of Steve. Then they're going to seal up my head with a titanium plate (sadly, adamantium is unavailable).*
>
> *Talk about shit I never thought I'd say: "I'm having brain surgery tomorrow" definitely belongs on that list.*
>
> *Regardless of the outcome—whether he's cancer or not— they'll likely never need to do more brain surgery.*

And if it is cancer . . . well, we'll burn that bridge when we come to it. Like I said, my tumor's small (only 1 cm), and he hasn't ventured into any other parts of my brain.

Still, we've been slightly on edge in my house about the whole brain tumor/brain surgery/brain cancer thing:

Me: *What if they botch my surgery?*

Rand: *They aren't going to botch your surgery.*

Me: *But what if they do. What if they accidentally hit the part of my brain that controls sarcasm. Or what if I wake up and I'm vapid?*

Rand: *You aren't going to wake up vapid.*

Me: *BUT WHAT IF I DO? What if I suddenly decide that Katherine Heigl is the greatest comedic genius to have ever lived, and I spend all my waking hours watching her movies? What if I start a fansite dedicated exclusively to her work?*

Rand: *Okay, that would actually be kind of amazing. I sort of want to see that happen.*

We've actually started taking turns freaking out. I mostly freak out about the surgery. Rand freaks out about the possibility of cancer:

Me: *Stop it. You're giving me that look.*

Rand: *What look?*

Me: *That oh-my-god-what-if-it's-brain-cancer look. It's sort of sad and weirdly probing. It's the look that everyone's been giving me lately.*

Rand: *I'm not giving you that look.*

Me: *Yes, you are. It's like you're trying to memorize my face. And then your chin starts getting all quivery. JUST LIKE IT IS NOW.*

Rand: *Well . . . what if it's brain cancer?*

Me: *It's not brain cancer. I'm not awesome enough to be diagnosed with something that dramatic.*

Rand: *That's the problem. You are precisely that awesome.*

Me: *Aww. That's sweet. I'd totally make out with you if you'd stop giving me that look.*

Rand: *I'm not giving you that look.*

Me: *YES YOU ARE.*

I was right: after the post went up, emails flooded in, as did comments. It was All About Steve. I read them at the kitchen table the day before my surgery, counting down the hours until the following morning. That night, I followed all the instructions Dr. Foltz gave me. I changed the sheets on the bed. I washed my hair with the runny pink soap. And the next morning, a little before 6 a.m., we headed to the hospital.

Rand drove me. Our friend Sarah—reassuring, logical, cracking the occasional joke—met us at the hospital. And my mother met us there, calm and smiling. All those years she'd spent worrying and instilling that worry in me had an unexpected upside: when shit actually does hit the fan, my mother is the picture of serenity. She is the one person you want in a crisis, because she's been preparing for it her entire life. She will make you food and clean your entire house and help you wash your hair with no discernable sign of stress on her face.

In times like this, my mother is perfect.

"I'm not nervous at all, sweetie, are you?" she asked. It had been more than ten years since that Florida trip, but my mother does not learn lessons. She was wearing half a dozen necklaces, several of them tangled in her long hair.

"I am," I said.

"It's going to be fine," she said, and the way she smiled at me, I believed every word.

One at a time, she and Rand and Sarah came in to see me as I got hooked up to an IV and changed into a gown. And then the nurse said it was time to go into surgery.

They wheeled me down a hall, where Dr. Foltz met us and chatted with me for a little bit. He asked how I was doing. Nervous, I told him. He said there was nothing to worry about.

"I'll see you in just a little while," he said, patting me on my shoulder.

As he walked away, I called out to him.

"Hey, Dr. Foltz," I shouted, and he turned around. I pointed to my head.

"Just a little off the top."

That would be the first and only time I ever got him to laugh. But he did, a soft little chuckle, more a shaking of his shoulders than anything else. It felt like a triumph, and that moment comes to mind every time I think about him. In exactly 364 days, on the eve of my first-year anniversary of brain surgery, my dear, stoic surgeon would succumb to a different cancer than the one he'd spent his career fighting.

I was wheeled into another room, large, sterile, and windowless. A handful of people lay in beds, waiting to be rolled into different operating rooms. Someone checked my IV. An old high school fling of mine (a young man I affectionately refer to as "the best sex I never had") had a friend who worked in the hospital who stopped by to say hello. Eventually, my anesthesiologist arrived and walked alongside my bed as we rolled toward the operating room.

"Am I going to be awake for much longer? Because I'm getting kind of nervous."

"I'll give you something for that right now," he said, and quickly injected a liquid into my IV. It took only a few seconds to work. When it did, the tiles on the floor started to change shape, growing smaller and bigger in front of my eyes.

Normally, I'm not down with visual hallucinations, but in this instance, I was rather okay with it. My fear felt small and distant; it didn't matter that the ground was now undulating.

Given the amount of drugs already in my system, I can't tell you for sure if my impression of the operating room itself was accurate. I remember it being massive, filled with all kinds of machinery—tubes and devices that would have scared me under normal circumstances.

"Is this all for me?" I asked, feeling bad that they had gone through all this trouble. Still wondering if it was at all necessary.

"Yup," someone responded. "All for you."

And then I closed my eyes.

✳ ✳ ✳

IN THE YEARS BEFORE RAND and I were married, he was on the road a lot. This would eventually become the impetus for my blog—I was traveling so I could see him. I *loved* seeing him. I loved the way his eyes crinkled when he smiled and

I loved his forearms when he rolled up his sleeves and I loved the way the mood of a room changed when he was around. It was like putting the final piece of a puzzle in place every time he walked in the door. When he was present, nothing was missing.

And when he was gone, it was like even the air and the trees and the sky knew that something was amiss.

Time on the road passed quickly for him, as it often does for overly busy people. He was trying to get the family business out of debt, attending and speaking at numerous conferences, running from meetings to industry events and darting from hotel to hotel. At home, working at a job I would soon lose, I spent a lifetime waiting for him to return. It always felt like something out of a science fiction novel—what had felt like only a few days for him was actually decades for me.

We started to have silly rituals before he was set to leave. Because the only thing worse than being madly in love with someone is being madly in love with someone who wasn't presently smothering you with affection. Sometimes, I'd fail to corral my tears and a few would escape from the corners of my eyes. I'd shake my head and smile at the ridiculousness of it all. And as if the utter nausea of our love story wasn't enough, sometimes he'd sing John Denver's "Leaving on a Jet Plane" right before he was set to depart.

I wish I could say that no part of it was earnest—we rolled our eyes at it, at this over-the-top melodrama at his own departure. It was just a few days, after all. I would pantomime barfing, much as I would on our wedding day. But if I am truly honest with myself, I know that all this posturing belied the sincerity at the heart of it. I meant every tear. He meant every word.

I've heard that after enough time, we can become accustomed to separation. That eventually, you cease to miss the person acutely. That never happened with Rand. I missed him constantly. With my job loss came a charmed opportunity to no longer be apart, and his company had experienced a blissful turn of fortune that meant we could afford to do it. I knew nothing about how to travel, I just knew that I wanted to be near him. He made the entire world feel like home.

I never went anywhere without him. Except when I had to.

My surgery became just another trip, but this time I was the one leaving. That was the easy part. It was always worse for the people you leave behind, the ones waiting for you to return. I just hoped I wouldn't be gone for very long.

11

BUCKET LISTS ARE JUST PLAIN GREEDY

I'VE NEVER REALLY BEEN A fan of bucket lists. They've always struck me as the height of entitlement. Admittedly, this is an odd perspective for me to have, as I have no problem placing demands on life. I think that dessert should be a daily occurrence, and I am absolutely convinced that there is someone out there for everyone, and that it's our mission on this earth to find them.

But for some reason demanding to see Angkor Wat before you died was too much for me. Too demanding. Too morbid. I figured you got what you got. It might be thirty-three years on this earth. It might be fifteen. It might be eighty-eight. Why couldn't we just enjoy them? Why did we feel the need to check things off as if existence was a to-do list?

Besides, there weren't things that I necessarily wanted to see. There were simply ways in which I wanted to live. Happily ever after, mostly, and without having to share too much of the afore-mentioned daily dessert.

So I rather proudly went through life without a bucket list.

Except for *one* nagging little thing. I'd first seen it in my middle school science book, in one of the chapters in the astronomy unit. It was a photo of the night sky with a thick, cloudy band of stars cutting across the middle of it, like a high-altitude bejeweled fog. The caption said that if you managed to escape light pollution you could see the arm of the Milky Way in which our solar system was located.

That photo, taken from Earth, gave an idea of where we sat in our galaxy.

Naturally, it blew my little middle-school-aged brain. For years, I thought about it, and it always remained in the back of my mind as something I'd love to see, but I wasn't going to write out my demands for the cosmos. I got a little paranoid thinking about what happened after they'd been met.

But as the years went by, I couldn't quite get the band of stars out of my head.

In college, I took an astronomy class at the University of Washington. The professor was a bespectacled blonde, pretty in that sort of hippie, earthy way women in the Pacific Northwest often are. Her name was Ana Larson.

Sometimes I'd play with the spacing of her name on my papers.

Ana L arson

Ana L Arson

I never actually got up the nerve to type "Anal Arson," but this exercise gave me a good giggle and an idea for what I suspect would have been the best-selling Nancy Drew mystery to date.

I should note, though, that this subtle defiling of her name did not mean she was a rotten teacher. She was wonderful. She conducted the stars like a concerto; I listened to every note. But she pronounced her name A-*nuh*, and when that sort of thing falls in your lap, you have to seize the moment even if it makes you an asshole.

Ana's class was at night, which was advantageous because that meant I was no longer hungover, but also problematic because *it was at nighttime in fall in Seattle*. For those uninitiated into the weather of my beloved hometown, imagine doing the Ice Bucket Challenge in pitch darkness. For nine months. And all the money raised goes to Satan.

Sometimes, when I was curled up in my tiny little studio apartment under a heap of blankets watching an episode of *Conan* that I'd taped the night before, not even her brilliance and passion could move me. Other times I'd drag myself out, trekking across a dark campus in the pouring rain, whispering to myself that there were far easier ways for a journalism major to earn the prerequisite science credits. But then I'd arrive in Ana's lecture hall, regretting nothing.

She showed us the heavens and the little corner of the universe that we occupied.

I was a passionate and nerdy student, or at least I was when I made it to class. I don't think Ana knew what to make of me. There were at least a hundred students enrolled, but I'd managed to single myself out as a target of both her praise and exasperation. She'd write notes on the board about upcoming classes and add in parenthesis, "EVERYONE must attend. Geraldine—this means YOU," and she'd give me sideways glances when I walked into the room half asleep in plaid pajamas.

But I aced every test, and I got a 4.0 in the class, and I think she realized that I loved the night sky almost as much as she did.

The class met in a massive auditorium, and every now and then, Ana would dim the lights and show us photos of the universe projected onto a giant screen behind her. I think part of the reason she always knew when I cut class and when I didn't was that I would *Oooh* and *Aaah* a little too loudly when a particularly captivating photo would go up. If the room was too quiet, she knew I was off-campus (usually eating microwave popcorn and marveling at the size of Conan's head).

Sure enough, one day she showed us one of those images, taken from some magical spot on Earth where you could see the arm of the Milky Way stretching across the sky.

My appreciation of the scene was perhaps a bit too loud. As I said: when I was in class, Ana knew.

During one lecture, she explained what would happen when our sun finally died out. How it would start to collapse on itself and would then swell, devouring the inner planets in the process. If the earth was not consumed, it would be charred to the point at which it couldn't sustain life.

"I know it's billions of years away," she said, "but it still makes me sad to think about it."

I would remember those words, would call on them when trying to articulate the reason why I hate bucket lists so much. I'm going to die. So are you, unless you're a vampire, or a zombie, or Keanu Reeves, whom age cannot wither. It's inevitable, and it's probably a good thing, because immortality would lead to all sorts of complications and I bet divorce rates would be even higher than they are.

If I'm lucky, it's a long way off. But it still makes me sad to think about it. And that's precisely what bucket lists *do*. They force you to look at wonderful experiences in the context of the *end* of your life, and not as a *component* of your life.

So I'd rather talk about the heyday—both the planet's and mine—of the time we get to spend basking in the sun's glow.

But in the week prior to my brain surgery, it seemed like all Rand and I could think about were things in this context. At one point, while my doctors were still discussing what the thing in my head might be (giving it a 10–20 percent chance of being brain cancer—numbers that are all at once strangely arbitrary and oddly specific), Rand sat down next to me and, with a far too serious look on his face, asked me what I wanted to do.

"I mean if it's cancer," he said. "What . . . do you want to do?"

"I am going to stop working out," I said. "And I'm going to eat cake every day."

He nodded gently. I'd been saying this for years. It had been a life goal long before I knew about my tumor.

"No, I mean, if it's cancer . . . is there stuff you want to see?"

He stopped there—no need to elaborate. My husband was asking me about my bucket list. Not in the abstract, not as a hypothetical, but in a very real, my-personal-sun-might-explode kind of way.

Over the years, the truth had leaked out about my astronomical passions. I was not spatially aware, but I loved space. I had no sense of direction, but I could pick out Polaris in the night sky.

When Rand learned of my celestial inclinations, he indulged them. He took me to the Hayden Planetarium in New York, to countless science centers and IMAX shows, to dark and distant spots far from city lights, all so I could see the stars.

There was always too much light pollution to see the band of the Milky Way, but that didn't really matter. I still had all those moments, and countless others. He'd ridden with me through the canals of Venice, had gotten lost on rainy streets in London looking for a well-hidden restaurant. We'd huddled together in a chilly cemetery in the Scottish highlands, and we'd scampered across Machu Picchu in the rain.

More things than I'd ever hoped to see. Far more than anyone could expect from their time on Earth.

And so, when Rand asked me what I wanted to do, assuming that the time I had might be less than we'd anticipated, I didn't think about it in terms of what I *hadn't* seen. I thought about all the things I had been lucky enough to witness.

And I answered him honestly.

"There's nothing left that I need to see."

There really wasn't.

I should clarify because that makes me sound like I was a lot braver than I was: I was petrified. I may have been blissfully content with my life, but that didn't mean I was okay with it being *over*.

There was still plenty more to see. The Northern Lights. The face of my nephew, who wouldn't be born for another month. A spread in *Vogue* magazine touting big noses as the next hot fashion trend for women. These were things I *wanted* to see.

But to *demand* them? To put them on a *list*? I couldn't do any of that. Because looking back on things, it was impossible not to be satisfied. I'd been to some amazing places. I'd seen some wonderful sights. And I'd done it with one hell of a travel partner. It's hard to ask for more than that.

* * *

I WAS IN THE RECOVERY room when Dr. Foltz came in and told me that my tumor had been a pilocytic astrocytoma, as he'd been 80 percent sure it was all along. Noncancerous, slow-growing, with a low rate of recurrence. The sun, it seemed, wasn't going to explode anytime soon. Under the influence of a narcotic that was ten times the strength of morphine, I could only nod. Rand was able to articulate his excitement more eloquently than I. When Dr. Foltz told him everything went well, Rand hugged him. He said he was pretty sure that he caught him by surprise when he did so, but my ever-serious doctor simply smiled.

Sometimes life gives you more than you deserve.

I reacted as you might expect. In the weeks following my surgery, I was ridiculously, stupidly happy, giddy just to be alive. Possessed with a sort of miraculous perspective on things. It didn't last (miraculous perspectives never do), but for a little while, everything made sense.

I didn't sweat the small stuff. I didn't care when strangers were rude, when someone cut me off in traffic. I was just incredibly excited to be awake and breathing and more or less whole, minus one noncancerous tumor and a nickel-sized piece of my skull. It made it very easy to focus on how beautiful and wonderful life is, how absurdly unlikely and magical existence can be.

It was not unlike the first time Rand took me to New York to see the Hayden Sphere at the Museum of Natural History. The sphere is massive—several stories tall, it fills up an entire hall in the planetarium section of the museum. There are little placards all around the giant orb, along with several much smaller spheres, that help you put the universe in perspective. If our sun were represented by the Hayden Sphere, with a diameter of eighty-seven feet, then the earth would be the size of a modest cantaloupe. At this scale, you can hold all of humanity in your hands.

When all of existence is condensed in such a way, the problems don't stand out. You can only marvel at the fact that there is an Earth filled with things like museums and cantaloupes and groups of screaming schoolchildren, and you feel so, so lucky that you get to be a part of it.

I wish I could say that it lasted and that I continued to understand the cosmos after I left the planetarium, but that wasn't how it worked. You go on with your life, and your newfound understanding of existence begins to leave you. By the time you hit Columbus Avenue you're back to worrying about if you can catch a cab and whether you can pull off a neoprene dress (the answer, in either case, is no).

Turns out, the epiphanies offered up by our experiences are temporary. The secrets that are revealed to you by the stars and the hole in your head begin to fade, and the wonder of being alive more or less goes away. I wish that it didn't. I wish I had remained forever grateful, forever able to keep things in perspective.

But every now and then, I can. I can look at the stars, and for a half second, it all makes sense.

Our first trip after my brain surgery was in early summer of 2012. We headed down to Ashland, the town in which we were married. It was part of an annual pilgrimage, one we took for our anniversary. That year, the staples were fresh out of my skull. I was still sleeping off the anesthesia and had to take a nap to make it through the day.

I don't remember that trip to Ashland well. Packing was confusing, and by the time I'd closed my suitcase, I'd forgotten what was inside. My face was still round from the steroids, my hair still greasy from whatever gel Dr. Foltz's assistant had put in it to keep it in place during the operation (several washes later, it still hadn't come out).

That miraculous perspective on life that surgery had granted me was already starting to fade. As more time passed, I found that I wasn't able to keep looking at everything from a distance, from so far away that the earth and my problems seemed small. I'd expected everything to change, and it hadn't. So I expected everything to go back to normal, but it didn't do that either. Those changes—even the ones I knew were small and likely temporary—loomed large in front of me, as if I were looking in a hotel magnifying mirror where everything is amplified and horrible and you are fairly certain you need a *Phantom of the Opera*-style mask to cover your acne scars. If I could only step far enough away, I'd know the greasy hair and the moon face and the sleeping for sixteen hours a day didn't matter. I was alive, and that should have been enough. But that's the problem with your own life: you are way too close to it to see it clearly.

What memories I do have of that trip to southern Oregon are a confusing patchwork. I know we saw an experimental play—*Medea, Macbeth, and Cinderella*. All three performances were staged simultaneously. It was sort of a brilliant, elaborately choreographed insanity. Following all the action on stage was impossible, and so you could only fixate on one small, incoherent thing at a time (the ghost of Banquo, for example, dancing with one of the stepsisters at the ball), which suited me just fine.

By the end, everyone was exhausted and confused; I was excited to have company, as this had been my mental state for the last week and a half. I remember our breakfasts at the Peerless Inn, which I devoured in massive bites, still ravenous from the steroids I'd had to take to stop my brain from swelling.

And I remember our trip to Crater Lake.

I don't know if Rand told me why we were going up there. I think he mentioned stargazing, but at no point did he say to me, "Hey, by the way, you're about to fulfill a lifelong wish." And I rather liked it that way.

Because I've found amazing things don't happen when you are trying to cross things off a list. Sometimes they just *happen*.

The lake is an hour and half from Ashland by car. We stopped only once on the way, when my steroid-induced hunger proved too much to wait for dinner, at Phil's Frosty, an ice cream stand halfway between Ashland and our destination. I got a scoop of mint chocolate chip ice cream to tide me over. It was gone by the time we pulled out of the parking lot.

I slept for much of the remainder of the journey, the road sun-dappled with bits of light that managed to sneak through the tall trees. At one point I lifted my head and made a half-hearted offer to drive, even though I could barely keep my eyes open.

Rand didn't laugh at the absurdity of the offer.

"Just sleep, kitten," he said. And I did, all the way to the lake.

Rand had taken me there nearly a decade before, on our first trip to southern Oregon, when we'd discovered Ashland for the first time. I remember being amazed when I first saw that lake— how brilliant and clear the water was. That afternoon it looked as blue as I remembered, more saturated and intense than even the cloudless sky above it.

The lake was formed when the top of the volcano Mount Mazama collapsed, leaving behind a large basin that filled with water. It is lined all the way around by the jagged sides of the volcano's mouth, a raised ridge with a dusting of trees on it, the only demarcation between the water and the sky.

The Crater Lake Lodge sits along this ridge, a stone-and-wood structure that looks at home here, where the forest and rocks and water meet. We had a dinner reservation there, but that was hours away, and so we wandered along the narrow hiking paths out front—flanked on either side by sharp cliffs that led down to the lake or down the side of the mountain.

I was still in the disaster-mode mind-set of my surgery—still not quite used to the fact that this wonderful life of mine was back in my hands—and whenever Rand stepped too close to an edge I'd beg him to move away, to step back onto the path. Occasionally I'd slip my fingers through his belt loops and lean backward, away from the cliffs, a counterbalance to the weight of his curiosity.

"You know that if I fell, doing that would just drag you with me, right?" he asked.

I nodded.

He finally relented and moved back on to the path. We walked, watching our shadows, linked at the hands, grow longer and longer on the dusty ground.

The sun began to set, the water and sky turning a deeper and deeper blue in almost perfectly coordinating shades, the jagged ring of mountain around the lake glowing orange with the fading light.

We wandered back into the lodge for dinner, another meal that I devoured while barely taking a breath. We chatted with a couple at a neighboring table. They were dark-haired and well-dressed and reminded me of some distant relatives in Italy. We discussed the meal and our lovely surroundings, how the lodge felt trapped in an earlier time. I don't remember it being entirely pertinent to the conversation, but at one point the gentleman explained that he had just gotten out of jail.

And I looked at him blankly before responding, "I've just had brain surgery." Which was even less pertinent to the conversation than his confession, but I thought we were all sharing.

He stared at me to see if I was joking, and I shrugged gently to assure him that I wasn't. Then we went back to our meals. When they left, he cast me a glance out of the corner of his eye, and a slight wave.

"That man just got out of prison," I said to Rand, who nodded gently. And I imagined that somewhere, that gentleman was talking to his dinner date and saying something along the lines of, "That woman just had brain surgery." And his date would nod, and all four of us would be thinking how strange the other's life was.

We stretched dinner out as long as we could. Nightfall is never in a hurry during a northwestern summer. And for once, miraculously, my perpetually busy husband was unhurried as well. Together, with nothing else to do, we waited for the sky to grow dark. There was still a bit of blue on the horizon at 10 p.m., and it was another half hour before the stars made their appearance.

Rand and I walked outside. The wind had picked up, and it sounded like crashing waves. It was colder than we'd anticipated. I pressed my palm gently against the hole in my head.

The nerves in my scalp had been cut, and now whenever I shivered it felt like a shock of electricity across my head, meeting at the site of my incision.

I was so fixated on this sensation that it wasn't until I heard Rand whisper a soft word of reverence that I turned my face upward to look at the sky.

It was everything the textbooks had promised.

The sky was crowded with stars so bright and numerous that they blended together in a shimmering haze. Most were concentrated in a wide band across the sky, a bright cloud of stars interspersed with a feathery dark fog that wove through it.

I was looking out onto our arm of the galaxy.

Rand pulled me near him and I stared up, over his shoulder, at the universe. We weren't out there long. It was cold, and late, and I was so tired that I could barely stand. I fell asleep soon after we climbed into the car for the long and lonely drive back to Ashland. But before I did, I craned my neck and looked up at the passing stars.

"I'd always wanted to see that," I said.

"I know."

"How'd you know?" I asked, as though it were some great mystery.

He laughed.

"Because you talk about it all the time."

On the night I saw the band of stars that I'd always wanted to see, I realized how unimportant that feat was. That it doesn't matter what we see while we're here. It makes no difference if there are twenty stamps in our passport, or two, or none.

What matters is that you find the right person with whom to spend your time on this earth. Someone who will take care of you when you are sick. Who will love you and the extra hole in your head. Who will drive for hours while you sleep in the passenger seat. Someone who will show you how immense the universe is and still make you feel that you are the brightest thing in the sky.

That's why I don't have a bucket list. Because I can't imagine asking the universe for more than that.

12

IS THERE A GAELIC WORD FOR "I'M FREAKED OUT ABOUT OUR MARRIAGE"?

I FILED AWAY MY BRAIN surgery—or I tried to. I needed to put the experience somewhere—perhaps a little box labeled "Steve"—it would fit tidily. I've always had a bit of an obsession with getting things in the right place. I think it's because I so rarely was.

I grew up in the 1980s, a sybaritic time before society realized that children needed to not spend their days eating sugar and watching movies in which Arnold Schwarzenegger killed things. There was a game those of my generation may remember called Perfection, which I'm convinced was simply a thinly veiled secret government experiment to see if panic attacks could be induced in six-year-olds.

Nearly all my neuroses may be traced back to this game (though being hepped up on Slurpees and pixie sticks for much of the Reagan administration probably did not help).

The game consisted of a variety of little plastic shapes that were designed to fit perfectly into a large plastic holder. A timer was set, and the goal was to get every piece into the right spot before it went off. If you failed to do so, the timer would screech loudly while all the pieces would violently pop out of the holder and you would simultaneously die of cardiac arrest.

I don't think I even owned this game. I probably played it only a handful of times at preschool, after which I spent the rest of the day shaking and singing the game's jingle to myself in a hoarse whisper.

I still remember the tune, which sounded suspiciously like "Pop Goes the Weasel":

> *Put the pieces into the slot*
> *Make the right selection*
> *But be quick you're racing the clock*
> *POP GOES YOUR CAROTID ARTERY!*

I may have some of the words wrong. It's been thirty years. But the warped lesson that the game instilled in me was this: everything has a place. Everything in your life needs to fit neatly into a little slot created just for it, and if it doesn't, everything will fall apart and your heart will explode.

This becomes a significant problem as you grow older and realize that not everything fits comfortably into one category or another. There are few true villains in our lives and few true heroes. Everyone is remarkably complicated in a way that fairy tales did not prepare us for. It would be so much easier if this weren't the case. If loved ones were infallible. If we never had to agonize over our own mistakes, because we never made any. If experiences and people and marriages could fit snugly into the "good" and "bad" categories.

Sometimes I wish I could have done that with our Ireland trip—that I could tuck it away in the "miserable" category, label someone the villain and write them and the trip off forever. But things are never that simple. To dismiss all of Ireland as a dark mark on our otherwise pristine travel record—a sacrificial trip to the gods that hold dominion over frequent flyers, necessary in order to keep everything else going smoothly—would be to do it a disservice. Good things happened there. And terrible things happened there. And good things emerged from those terrible things. And now I have a headache.

Besides, if I were to name a villain, there's a good chance it would be me.

And so the entire trip floats in my mind, with no distinct schema in which to place it. It remains murky and confusing. There is no perfection here. Only the complicated reality of life, of relationships, of two very sad people trying to figure out their unhappiness and occasionally forgetting one another in the process.

It seems fitting that all that should happen in Ireland. That we would find ourselves in turmoil and conflict on an island that has been rocked by those things over the last century. (I don't mean to make light of Ireland's past by comparing it to my marital strife. Only to stress that some places have endured so much human suffering they can easily absorb whatever small grief you throw at them.)

Let's begin with a brief history lesson.

There are two entities that answer to the name of Ireland. Some will argue that this is how it should be. Others will argue that there is only one Ireland, and it's only a matter of time before the political situation reflects that truth.

They are both found on the same island, the only line of demarcation being an imaginary one decided upon nearly a century ago that remains hotly—and sometimes violently—debated.

Northern Ireland, composed of six counties in the northwest of the country, is part of the United Kingdom. The Republic of Ireland—an independent country that uses an entirely different currency—comprises the rest of the island.

The Republic of Ireland was established in the 1920s. Prior to that, the entire island was under British rule. It came in the wake of centuries of fighting and culminated in the Easter Rising—an attempt to declare independence from England that ultimately failed, resulting in the imprisonment of more than thirty-five hundred Irishmen and -women and the execution of fifteen revolutionary leaders.

News of their mistreatment and deaths swayed a large portion of the public that had previously not been in support of independence. Seeing that the protests (and the ensuing violence) would likely not end, England offered a treaty that relinquished control of most of Ireland—but withheld the six northern counties where the majority of the population supported unification with Britain.

The problem was that not everyone agreed with the treaty. Many felt that the entire island of Ireland should be its own country, including a number of people who lived in those northern counties that remained under British rule. This created a schism between factions—primarily in Northern Ireland—that still exists, often falling along religious lines. (The majority of people in the Republic of Ireland are Catholic. Those in

Northern Ireland are mostly Protestant.) This conflict is the heart of what is known as the Troubles.

The city of Belfast remains so divided that massive "peace walls" run through it—separating Catholic and Protestant neighborhoods that align themselves on opposite sides of the reunification debate. The walls—massive, imposing, and lined with barbed wire at the top—cut through the city, defying their name by their very nature.

Two Irelands, occupying the same island, divided by conflict. That is the setting in which we found ourselves. Beginning in Belfast, a city still haunted by the bombings that tore it apart at the height of the Troubles, we found ourselves there for remarkably happy reasons.

Our friend Ciaran was getting married. An Englishman with an Irish moniker and a Protestant family was marrying a Catholic woman from Ireland, both of them absurdly and blissfully in love and a reminder that no conflict is insurmountable.

Rand had met Ciaran first, years ago at a conference in London, and we'd become friends. We didn't see him all that often, and though his lines in the drama of our lives were few, he would become a major player. Enter stage left, dramatically change the course of the plot, and leave stage right. Only a few scenes, but afterward, nothing was the same.

He is aridly sarcastic, perpetually annoyed, and altogether charming. Blue-eyed, tall, suffering from a rather acute case of excessive handsomeness, albeit in a buttoned-up kind of way. Not quite James Bond but possibly his accountant.

The first time I spent any real amount of time with him was in the spring of 2008 in Sydney, Australia. It was one of the first big trips I'd taken with Rand, and I knew he was going to be busy with work, so I, recently laid off, planned on locking myself in the hotel room, watching Aussie soap operas, and eating koala-shaped chocolates until he was free in the evening.

Ciaran would have none of that.

"This is my favorite city in the world," he said, "so under no circumstances are you allowed to hang around here while I'm stuck in a conference. *Go*," he pointed to the lobby door. "Get out of here."

Petrified, as any American is by the inherent authority that seems to accompany the English accent, I obeyed. (Turns out, I was more scared of Ciaran's scolding than I was of losing my way.) I went to the Sydney Opera House, got lost on some quay (as usual), and took a ferry across the harbor until I spotted something that looked vaguely familiar. For roughly three blocks, I discreetly followed a group of gentlemen I thought were members of the Australian Olympic swim team (parenthetically, I would like to take this moment to note that I love my husband dearly and that sixpacks are probably overrated).

It was the first time I'd ever ventured out in a foreign city on my own. So without much hyperbole I can say that part of the reason my blog exists is Ciaran forcing me out onto the streets of Sydney by myself all those years ago.

I remember when I first told him about the Everywhereist.

"I have good news," I said excitedly.

"You *do* have a sister?" was his swift reply.

My response to this unexpected compliment was an elegant snort followed by a gurgling sound, not unlike the mating calls of certain types of swamp creatures, after which I hid behind Rand and refused to speak.

"Well done," my husband noted of either my reaction or the comment that elicited it—I cannot say which.

After hearing about my tumor, Ciaran sent me a note that said, simply, "I hope you are well. Please note that brain surgery in no way exempts you from being at my wedding."

His wedding was two short months after my surgery; I promised him we'd be there. And so, that September, we crossed the Atlantic to watch him cast aside the shroud of grumpy old man that he wore so well and to briefly allow us to see him young, happy, and in love.

It's strange to think of a happy event that takes place during a difficult time in your life. It stands out, it shines brightly against the darkness around it, but it does not remain untouched. The sadness infuses it. You are left wanting to laugh and cry all at once. Not everything has its own spot.

During this time I was still plagued by headaches, which seemed even worse than before—it felt as if they were emanating straight from the hole in my skull and left me feeling like my head had been cleaved in two (arguably, I suppose, it had). I felt isolated from people around me, separated by the unique experience of having my head cut open, unable to discuss my lingering problems when they were so relieved that I was fine and they were ready to move on. They would stare at my face, searching for hidden signs of illness, while I tried to look as normal as possible in hopes of passing the test.

I couldn't commiserate with other people I knew who had gone through brain surgery, because my case was so minor compared to theirs. They had had numerous surgeries and harrowing recoveries; they had lived with MRIs for years. A select few had brain cancer. I had no right to feel kinship with them when my outlook was so rosy.

I had no reason to be miserable, and yet I was, and my self-pity sickened me. All in all, not a great chapter in the book of

Geraldine. But there were other stories to be told, like Ciaran's. And Rand's.

The ceremony was in the Republic of Ireland, and the reception was in Northern Ireland. We crossed that invisible boundary from one to the other on winding roads that left me reeling, depositing the contents of my stomach on the side of the road. I felt a perverse pride at throwing up *before* an Irish wedding, and I tried to laugh off my nausea but wondered if there wasn't more to it. If there wasn't something inherently wrong with me, something that couldn't be cut out of my brain. If I was broken, and no amount of surgeries could fix me.

I wanted to be the sort of person who could have a drink and eat some chocolate and not keel over with head-splitting migraines. Who didn't constantly feel sick or foggy-headed. Who wasn't so damn high-maintenance.

I curled up on the bed in our rental cottage while Rand whispered that we didn't need to go to the reception. I shook my head, dizzy and determined. I brushed my teeth and walked on unsteady feet to the party, leaning heavily on his arm.

My stomach still tender, I drank two ginger ales and picked at the gourmet meal brought to us by men in white coats. But by the time that dessert was served, I was well enough to eat mine and most of Rand's. (A blissful discovery: in England and Ireland, both dessert and wedding cake are served. A less blissful one: the latter is a Christmas-style fruit cake and is usually terrible.)

I met the bride, bright eyed and stunning, who crouched down next to me, her white dress billowing around her as she inquired about my health. I smiled at what a miraculous thing it was—that on her wedding day, she was pausing to ask me, a stranger up until that moment, about my surgery. Smitten, I told her I was fine.

And at that moment, surrounded by friends, I was. There was only dancing and too much drinking and stealing puffs of forbidden cigarettes and photos of us looking dapper and lovely. For a little while, it almost seemed like everything was in its right place, before the pieces scattered and I wondered if we'd ever be able to get them back where they belonged.

We remained in that sleepy village for a few days longer before returning to Belfast, Rand growing increasingly stressed as time went by. Ireland was supposed to be the first real vacation that he had taken since our own wedding four years earlier. That had been his intention all along—but reality wasn't aligning. His email was piling up, and coworkers were writing him with increasing urgency.

In the time that I had known him, my husband had taken a struggling tech company mired in half a million dollars of debt and turned it into a multimillion-dollar success. His name appeared on countless rankings—the Top 30 Entrepreneurs Under 30, *Inc. Magazine*'s Fastest-Growing Companies—and in the occasional hilarious listicle, like "The 10 Hottest Male Geeks on the Web." (I emailed the latter to friends, laughing maniacally, while Rand cringed.) He worked constantly. On the road, at home, on weekends. He was up until 2 a.m. most nights typing away.

He skipped parties and social events to deal with his never-ending work obligations, came home late and ate dinner in a rush before running back to his computer. In recent years, I'd watched the hair over his temples turn gray, watched dark circles take up permanent residence underneath his eyes.

His coworkers once threw him a birthday party at his office and invited me. We all gathered and sang happy birthday as Rand stepped out, thanked everyone, blew out the candles, and went straight back into his office. Someone pulled out a life-size cardboard cutout of him, a joke prop made for another event he couldn't attend, and we pretended to feed it cake and snapped photos with that, instead.

I had approached his busyness with varying degrees of acceptance over the years. I figured it was temporary, and I figured he enjoyed it. I knew we were absurdly fortunate how things had turned out. I was able to follow him around the world, to visit friends in far-off places, to live comfortably. But recent months had left him sick and exhausted, unable to sleep, occasionally unable to even walk because of the shooting pain in his back and leg that was exacerbated by stress. If he caught a cold, it would last for months.

He needed a break, was pleading for one, and I was incapable of understanding why he didn't just take one. It was *his* company. I failed to understand that being the boss didn't allow that. For the last few months, when the stress and pain was so intense that he couldn't sleep, he would tell me that he'd get a break in Ireland. It became a sort of mantra.

It wasn't until we returned to Belfast, after the wedding, that I found out Rand had booked three speaking engagements over the course of our trip. He had yet to build presentations for two of them.

I found myself sputtering with rage, angry in a way that surprised both of us. I had always been his advocate but suddenly found myself on the attack.

"*You're* the one who said you needed to relax."

"I know, I know. I'm sorry."

"Why are you apologizing to me? Apologize to yourself," I snapped.

Rand and I rarely fight. We used to, in the early years of our relationship. The kind of tearful, exhausting arguments that lasted so long that by the end we'd forgotten what we were upset about. The kind you can only have when you are in your early twenties and scared to death by your own feelings.

But at some point, we stopped. I think we just realized it was pointless. We always made up, anyway, so it seemed easier just to skip to that part. And I labeled the laundry hampers, so he started putting his dirty clothes in the correct ones, which eliminated roughly 90 percent of all conflicts we had, anyway.

In Ireland, though, things were different. For the first time in our relationship, I didn't see a resolution. I tried to skip to it—but couldn't. I imagined him working like this until he died or our marriage fractured from the weight of it. My rage only served to magnify the problem. Rand was now overworked and felt guilty about it. He tried to divide his time in Ireland—attempting to appease work and me, and succeeding at neither.

We took a black cab tour across Belfast, walked through neighborhoods separated by barbed wire and ideology and violence until we were numbed by the sheer devastation of conflicts immeasurably greater than ours, before Rand would run back to the hotel to do more work. We rented a car and drove to the Giant's Causeway, a geological marvel of basalt rock formations on the coast. They look like giant stacks of stone scones. Or maybe they don't at all, and I was just hungry.

The drive there is supposedly one of the prettiest in the world. Rand was behind the wheel, driving on the left side of the road, and trying to operate a stick shift after watching exactly one instructional video on YouTube, which I will tell you now is not at all sufficient. Under different circumstances, we'd have laughed. But where we now found ourselves, neither of us did. I took it as a sign that he couldn't understand when he'd reached his limits. That he couldn't say no.

He took it as a sign that no matter how hard he tried, it would never be enough.

We climbed around the Giant's Causeway, tried to take self-portraits for my blog, a site built around our unassailable marriage. I smiled and felt like a fraud. Leaned in to kiss him as he stared at me, wounded and wide-eyed, wondering if this meant he was forgiven. I didn't know the answer any more than he did.

The time we spent together cut directly into his working hours, leaving him even more stressed and panicked. There was no way out.

"I don't understand. I'm usually working when we're on the road. I don't get why this trip is different."

"Because this was supposed to be a vacation," I told him. "This was supposed to be you taking a break."

We took the train to Dublin, barely speaking on the ride down. It was too dark to see anything outside—only indiscernible shapes on the landscape. Houses, hills, trees—I couldn't tell. Nothing makes sense in the dark.

In Dublin we toured the Guinness Brewery, a place Rand had excitedly talked about visiting before the trip. Twenty minutes after we arrived, after a few panicked glances at his watch, he explained that he had to go.

"I need to work on my presentation."

I heaved a sigh and followed him out of the building, despite his insistence that I stay. Wandering through a brewery alone while crying seemed like it might be kind of a buzzkill for the other tourists.

We parted ways on the street, a quick, terse goodbye, a perfunctory peck on the cheek before I watched him quickly disappear down an incongruously sunny street, his pace quick, punctuated by a slight limp, a result of his aggrieved and aching back.

Left alone on the winding streets of Dublin's trendy Temple Bar neighborhood, I enjoyed the sickening gratification that comes from wallowing in your own sadness. I suspect I'm not alone in this phenomenon. It's why people keep buying those books by Nicholas Sparks in which all the beautiful people die. My mind leapt to dramatic ends; I envisioned decade after decade of Rand slowly killing himself with work, of me fighting to get his attention, struggling to get time on his calendar to remind him of my existence.

And then I tried to imagine a future without the person with whom I'd spent the last decade. I realized the paradox at the heart of it—that my response to not seeing enough of Rand was to entertain a reality where I didn't see him at all. I obsessed on this idea until I was near panic, then slowly pulled myself back from hysteria and returned to the familiar comfort of my rage.

I thought he was doing it to himself. I didn't realize that he felt trapped, unable to extricate himself from something that had grown bigger than he knew how to wield. That he felt like it all rested on his shoulders—that if he failed, he would bring down every single person who worked for him. Stepping back or working less or doing something else were not options. I didn't understand that he was drowning. I was just angry at him for not being able to breathe.

So I twisted the narrative until it made sense to me—until I became the victim. I told myself that if he really loved me, he would be able to take a break. To put us above his work. He'd done that, briefly, in the days before my surgery. He done it when he thought that there was something wrong with me, and now that he thought I was fine, I'd lost him again. I hated myself for not being enough for him. I hated myself for being miserable despite an enviable life and a cancer-free brain.

There was no resolution in Ireland. Belfast remains divided by its barbed-wire walls, the Emerald Isle cut in two by national boundaries. I wondered if Rand and I would make it. Memories of the trip exist, both sad and happy ones, inextricably mixed together. I can't put anything in its designated spot. The pieces were scattered, and my heart felt like it might tear in two.

13

SALVATION LOOKS A LOT LIKE WISCONSIN

THERE ARE NO SIMPLE FIXES. When I tell you that things turned out well, that Rand would emerge from his cloud of depression and anxiety and find some sort of balance between work and life, know that it did not happen quickly or easily. The path out of darkness looks different for everyone. It may be paved with religion, or meditation, or therapy, or antidepressants, or (god help us all) *regular exercise.*

Sometimes the path is remarkably steep—a quick ascent that pulls you out of the gloom quickly, but leaves you so tired that you need to curl up on the coach for several long weeks watching Cary Grant movies in order to recover. Other times the rise is so gradual, you barely notice it, until one day you get out of bed and realize you're okay. The road may be twisting and riddled with bumps and potholes, or straight and smooth.

Rand's looked miraculously like the quiet stretch of highway between Milwaukee and Green Bay, Wisconsin.

Make no mistake: it was more complicated than a simple drive. It was a sad and complex journey, one that required doctor's visits and therapist visits and difficult discussions with numerous boards of directors. But it was on that stretch of road that Rand and I realized he—and we—might be okay.

It was the fall of 2012, not long after our Ireland trip and Ciaran's wedding. We'd spent the weeks in between walking on eggshells around one another. Rand was still working panicked hours, still sputtering apologies as he left the dinner table, his meal only half finished, to spend the rest of the evening locked away in his office.

"Why can't you just have an affair like everyone else?" I'd shout at him in some pitiful attempt at jocundity; we'd both try to laugh. I used to describe his company as the other woman. In recent months, I'd stopped.

"I'm the one sneaking around, begging for your time," I said. "*I'm* the other woman."

We tried to joke about it, ignoring the fact that he still wasn't sleeping, still spent his nights either on his feet in front of a glowing screen or tossing in bed, unable to find a position in which his leg and back didn't hurt.

But other than putting on brave faces, we still hadn't done anything to fix things.

"You're coming with me to Milwaukee, right?" he asked me tentatively one afternoon.

My presence on his trips had not been a guarantee in recent months. But he now had a conference in Wisconsin, a state I couldn't even pinpoint on a map, and it sounded strangely exotic to me. This is what happens when you are a first-generation American—certain parts of the country remain foreign to you. The Midwest holds a sort of strange mystique. There were entire families there that had been in the United States for generations, people who could trace back their roots to the Mayflower. Homes where everyone spoke the same language.

That there was a part of my home country stranger to me than Europe itself was utterly mind-blowing; I wanted to see it. Plus, I was curious as to what exactly fried cheese curds were, because I wasn't entirely clear on that point. I told Rand I'd go with him.

"Maybe we could even go up to Green Bay," he said, his eyes bright.

For as long as I had known him, my husband had been a football fanatic. His favorite team was, somewhat inexplicably, the Green Bay Packers, a town and an institution to which he had no inherent attachment. Rand's family is from New York, and he was born in Jersey, but he's always had an affinity for a team whose fans are known for wearing giant Styrofoam cheeses on their heads. I've always found this facet of Wisconsin fandom fascinating.

"What's our mascot?"

"The Packers."

"Excellent. BRING ME A HAT THAT LOOKS LIKE CHEESE."

Before I continue, let me be clear about something: I don't like the National Football League. It's inherently misogynistic: there are no female commentators except for a few on-field, and it was only in 2015 that the first female referee was hired. The organization has been horrifically silent on issues of domestic

abuse perpetuated by its players off-field and seems woefully unconcerned about the players' health on-field. Players regularly
get concussions—or worse—but the legacy of brain damage
from such collisions remains altogether ignored.

I've noted that there would be far fewer instances of neurological damage if the athletes played without helmets, padding,
and maybe even shirts, but thus far my suggestions have gone
unheeded by the NFL.

Rand, I should note, agrees with me on all this (though he's
not quite as adamant about the whole shirtless thing).

Despite all that, the Green Bay Packers may have saved my
marriage. I realize the absurdity of that statement, but I know
people who credit Ultimate Frisbee with their domestic bliss,
who attribute their happiness to Magic: The Gathering or intra-
mural soccer or trivia night at the neighborhood bar. Salvation
can be found in the most unlikely places. Like on the stretch of
highway between Milwaukee and Lambeau Field.

I knew Rand wanted to visit the home stadium of his favorite team, but I assumed that, like so many other things,
he'd have to skip it in favor of work. I was pleasantly surprised,
though still somewhat incredulous, to find that on his work trip
he booked an extra day just to drive up to Green Bay.

For the first time that I could remember, Rand was doing
something he wanted to do. I drove, not making a sound, afraid
to break the spell, while he took an assortment of phone calls.

Someone once told me that I only endured football because
of Rand, and I wanted to laugh, because it's not like he's particularly enjoyed the countless seasons of *American Idol* that I made
him sit through while I did interpretive dances to the songs
in various states of undress. Sometimes something becomes

important to you because it's important to the people you love. Like sports, or terrible reality TV shows, or adhering to local nudity laws.

The road was flat, the early October sky clear and blue. By the time we pulled into the stadium parking lot, Rand was excitedly bouncing in his seat. I love moments like that, when you realize you are married to a giant, human-shaped puppy. I had to be careful he didn't run into the traffic the second the door opened.

I once asked Rand about his affinity for the Packers.

"I'm a socialist," he said, brightly, referring to the fact that there is no billionaire at the helm of Green Bay's team. The club is a nonprofit that is owned by the town, the nuances of which were explained to us by our guide during the ninety-minute-long tour. I listened intently while watching Rand have the closest thing to a religious experience that I'd ever seen him have. He gingerly touched the walls of the stadium and stepped with utter reverence over the tiles on which generations of Packer players had crossed. He delicately tried on jerseys in the gift shop as though they were made of silk, finally selecting one that he wore out of the store.

For the first time in a very long time, Rand was doing something *he* wanted to do.

On the ride back to Milwaukee, after a lunch consisting of fried cheese curds followed by a side of dietary regret, Rand took one more call while I drove. It was with a therapist who had been recommended to him by a colleague. I hadn't anticipated this.

I listened while Rand relayed to him everything that had happened in Ireland and everything that had happened at work that led to that breaking point.

The trees on the side of the freeway were beginning to change color as I listened to my husband admit he was overwhelmed. How he constantly felt like he was behind. He told him about his chronic pain and his inability to sleep. How he felt that he couldn't take time off because doing so would mean letting his coworkers down. The therapist asked him how he'd feel if his coworkers said something like that to him.

Terrible, Rand admitted. But he had more at stake in the company. He *had* to be the hardest-working person there.

"Yeah, but how can your coworkers comfortably take a break if they don't see you doing it?"

Rand had no reply to that.

The therapist then gave him a homework assignment: Rand and I would talk about the lack of balance in his life, how it made us both feel, and what we could do to fix that.

On the drive back, after a day spent at Lambeau Field, as the sun was setting and the sky over the surprisingly flat state of Wisconsin began to glow a soft peach hue, we had that talk. I told him how it seemed like work came before everything. How it felt that he never prioritized us. How he never even prioritized himself.

I told him how the only time I had felt important to him was before my surgery, leaving me nostalgic for a terrible time in my life. How now that I was okay, work went back to being first on his list.

"I felt like you were just waiting to go home every night from the hospital so you could work," I said.

How I had come to this conclusion was unclear to me—I scarcely remembered my hospital stay. But somehow, I'd managed to form hurt feelings while barely conscious. I held a grudge even though I had forgotten nearly everything that happened.

"Baby," Rand said, "that's not true. I just went home and slept. And every morning, I came back to the hospital to be with you."

And then: "You are more important than work."

Deep down, I'd known this. But upon hearing it vocalized, I promptly started to cry. This is slightly problematic when one is driving on the freeway. I wiped my eyes with the back of one hand while I steered with the other. I began to realize that the source of my own unhappiness was not exclusively my overtaxed marriage. It was because my head still hurt and his back always did. It was because I felt alone and he felt overwhelmed. While Rand was mired in stress, I'd created a false narrative—one in which I was unloved and uncared for, his work would always take precedence over us, and he saw no reason to change things because I—and our relationship—just were not worth it. Especially now. Especially with a hole in my head.

But during that drive, I realized that the endless hours he spent working had nothing to do with me. It had to do with him.

We started talking about what we could do to fix things. We made a list of all the stuff we wanted to change. One day a week, Rand would come home before 7 p.m., and he wouldn't work on his computer again until the next morning (it has since been known as "anti-work night" and is a recurring appointment on his calendar). He promised to take a vacation, during which he'd work less than sixty minutes a day. Eventually, he might limit his work on one weekend day to less than one hour.

I, in turn, promised not to run into his office in my underwear and scream "BREAKTIME!" while pouring a gallon of bleach over his laptop.

In the coming months, Rand would achieve most of his goals. He started saying "no" more. He hired an assistant who is kind and capable and makes sure he doesn't die of dehydration. He would eventually voluntarily step down as CEO, instead crafting a role for himself in which he works on the projects and products he wants to and travels around the world, speaking and building brand awareness. These were all positive steps toward achieving real balance in his life.

And then, perhaps most remarkable of all, Rand took a vacation.

He got away from work for a while. Really, really far away. Rand, never able to underachieve, put the entire planet between himself and his office. Two months after our trip to Green Bay, in January 2013, we went on vacation in South Africa, which is Seattle's antipode—the point on the globe that was farthest away from it. Or, rather, South Africa is very close to being the antipode—the actual spot is in the middle of the Indian Ocean. If you find it on a globe, you will see that it is surrounded by lots of blue enamel paint.

Approximately 160 miles northeast of Cape Town is Bushmans Kloof, a lodge located in the middle of a wilderness retreat. It was here, in a remote part of a country on the other side of the world from home, that things started to change. That was where we saw the animals. The Kloof is home to thousands of them.

Every night guides would take us out on wilderness drives in search of creatures to spy on. Because the reserve was fenced

in and there were no predators, the animals we saw weren't ter-
ribly skittish. They just stood in the golden fields, eating and
staring at us. A lot of the time, we were doing the same thing.

Here's the thing about Rand: he adores animals. I've seen
him scamper over rocks in pursuit of lizards and sit motionless
by the side of a pond in hopes that a frog might appear. We once
came across a turtle in a creek, and for the rest of the day Rand
talked about it.

"Wasn't that a great turtle?" he asked me, and I wanted to
tell him that I had no idea whether it was or not—I had no
frame of reference as to what made a turtle great. These are
things that are beaten out of you—sometimes literally—in middle school. Somehow, Rand who always, always had to be the
grownup, had managed to hang on to this one glorious facet
of childhood—an absolute love for the grimy, slimy natural
world.

When I saw the look of utter delight on his face at the mere
memory of that turtle, there was no other answer for me to give
other than the affirmative.

"That was the best turtle ever," I said.

"Well, I wouldn't go *that* far."

At the Kloof, it was like that every day. Our turtle pond
overfloweth. We saw zebras, wildebeests, ostriches, and a
number of creatures that we'd never even heard of before visiting South Africa. Oryx. Bonteboks. Elans. Red hartebeests.
Giraffippos.

(Okay, I made that last one up. We're getting to the end of
the book. I just wanted to see if you were still paying attention.)

On top of all those, I saw what may have been the most elusive creature of all. I saw my husband, relaxed. He slept in. He

didn't check his email. He tried sneaking up on a herd of elan and found a gecko living under the light fixture on the balcony of our cottage.

One night, he looked at me as we were watching the sun set over a ridge and said, "You know what? My back doesn't hurt. That hasn't happened in four years."

Under a blue African sky, the freckles on his nose came out and the crease in his brow began to slowly fade. He laughed, and we made memories and the world back home did not fall apart.

And then, after several sunlit days on the other side of the earth, we went back to Seattle.

I won't pretend that everything is fixed. Changes to the patterns of your life take time. The masterpieces of the world—Rome and the pyramids and Jeff Goldblum's abs—were not built in a day. Rand still frantically rushes around, still doesn't sleep regular hours, still works weekends. His hair continues to turn gray; his back continues to hurt.

But sometimes, sometimes, he steps away from it all. He takes a break. He sits down and enjoys himself and watches a football game. He reads a book. Sometimes, we go somewhere and look for frogs.

Every now and then, he does the things that he wants to do. Those trips—whether across the world or down the road—are always my favorite ones.

Rand once told me that you can't engineer quality time. You can only spend a lot of time with someone and hope that it turns into that. That if you are lucky, something memorable will happen. Our journey out of the dark could have taken place at any point along our travels. Or it might not have happened at all.

The location, if I'm truly honest with myself, had nothing to do with it. But I remember exactly where we were when Rand, for the first time, perhaps ever, started to put himself first. And for the first time, ever, I put him first, too. These two trips—disparate and unalike but forever tied together in my memory—are when I first started to think that he, and we, would be okay.

14

TURNS OUT, THINGS AREN'T ALWAYS WHAT THEY SEEM

IT SEEMED LIKE THINGS SHOULD have been okay after that. My marriage was on the mend. Rand was working less. My tumor wasn't cancerous. I should have been happy.

Let me tell you something that is not at all surprising but nevertheless came as a bit of a shock to me.

Brain surgery is a very, very big deal.

You're probably thinking, *Really? You didn't see that coming? That someone carving into your head and taking out bits of it might be a very special sweeps week–worthy episode of your life, like that time on* Friends *when Winona Ryder kissed Jennifer Aniston?*

And no, I did not. I can be shockingly obtuse when it comes to matters of my own life. It's why I keep buying jumpsuits, despite the fact that they're the adult equivalent of a onesie. You can glimpse so many of the treasures that the world has to offer, you can study its mysteries and its secrets, yet the ability to see yourself clearly, and to realize that certain clothing makes you look like a giant toddler, will continue to elude you.

The significance of my brain surgery and the difficultly of the ensuing recovery caught me by surprise. Because it wasn't actually brain cancer and because structurally my brain was healthy (despite vast swaths of it being dedicated to the plots of 1990s-era sitcoms and the names of every member of the Wu-Tang Clan, living or dead), I'd managed to convince myself that was the end of the story.

During my surgery, ten staples had been placed in my head while I was still under—a neat little row holding my scalp together. An eleventh went in when I was conscious, cutting through the haze of painkillers to make me wince. The technician apologized profusely.

"This is why everyone hates me," she said, pitifully.

"It's okay," I lied. She must have been terrible at parties.

Ten days after my surgery, those metal brackets were removed in a series of surprisingly painless snaps, and I reasoned that was sufficient time for me to get back to normal. Or whatever passes for normal for someone who insisted that she wanted photos of Patrick Stewart on her business cards so that she could hand them to people and say, "My Pi-*card*."

I'd be back to that, *right*?

But that isn't what happened.

I passed my neurological tests with flying colors. I was able to squeeze the doctor's fingers on cue, could follow the little light that they waved in front of my eyes, and could relay the president's name when asked.

But I felt different.

"Something's changed," I'd tell Rand, after spending far too long in front of the bathroom mirror, staring at a reflection that seemed slightly off, as though someone had tried to recreate my face from memory and hadn't quite gotten all the details right.

"Nothing's changed."

"I look different."

"Nope."

"My face. It's different now."

"It's the same one you had before."

Frustrated that he was unable to see the utterly intangible but still fucking obvious thing in front of him, I'd insist that I *felt* different, knowing that this was an impossible point for him to argue.

He never lost his patience during my many attempts to get him to admit that I was changed, never gave any fuel to my growing notions that I was different now, less lovable. But if you repeat any notion enough you risk it becoming true, no matter how absurd. Kale chips are delicious. Leggings may be worn in place of pants. We are not deserving of love or kindness.

Yet even as my neuroses pushed my beliefs to the border of becoming self-fulfilling, I was adored. When I would insist that I was no longer myself, Rand would stop whatever he was doing to wrap his arms around me—long, blanketing embraces meant to calm the demons inside me, well-intended but entirely ineffectual.

"You had brain surgery," he'd say. "Give it time."

Patience is a profoundly difficult thing to have when all you want is to feel like yourself again.

In the last few years, I'd come to terms with the idea of getting lost as I made my way around the world. I could handle taking the wrong train or making a wrong turn, realizing that in either case I'd be fine. I'd be in Queens when I meant to go to Chelsea, but I'd be fine.

What I was not okay with was feeling disoriented in places I knew well. At home, or in front of a computer, or inside my own head. I was fine if the world around me was unfamiliar, but it was a different matter entirely when *everything I was* started to feel that way, too.

I began to scrutinize every aspect of myself. My voice, which sounded more shrill and more nasal than I remembered. My jawline, which looked weirdly fleshy, as though the moon face from the steroids I'd taken had never really gone away.

And something else less tangible than even those things. Something indescribable that had made me who I was seemed irrevocably different. I was okay with losing my keys and losing my way and losing a chunk of my skull, but I was terrified at the prospect of losing myself.

I've never had much trouble making conversation. I could walk into a room of strangers and introduce myself to them without thinking twice about it. It was something I prided myself on, a necessary skill I'd honed when traveling with Rand to professional events. He'd get pulled away by someone who was eager to discuss something involving acronyms, and so I'd roam the room engaging people in conversation while I made my way to the dessert buffet. Part of this was tactical: if you head straight for the cake table at a party to which you are not technically invited, security is occasionally called. But if you ask people about their lives and their children along the way, no one will call you out when you go back for sevenths.

And part of it was simply this: I like people. I like learning about their go-to karaoke songs and their favorite bad movies and seeing photos of their sticky toddlers. These things are important.

But after my surgery, I felt like I'd lost that part of myself (the conversational part, I mean. My lifelong quest for cake endured and was arguably now less hampered by human interaction, but I would still argue that something essential to who I was had gone missing). The ease with which I once composed concertos of conversation was gone. I tripped over phrases; I struggled with small talk. Cognitive exercises that had once seemed effortless—like blogging, and tweeting, and fighting with people on the Internet who used "literally" improperly—were now frustrating at best. On bad days, they were impossible.

I'd stare at my computer screen, the cursor flashing at me like a metronome. I'd tap along, trying to will the words out, but they never came.

I wondered if they'd escaped, rushing out of the hole in my head. Or if my tumor itself had been some integral part of who I was. I mean, you can't take out a piece of someone's brain and have them be the same.

Or can you?

But every checkup I had was perfect. My brain was utterly undamaged. No one noticed any differences, or if they did, they said nothing. All of this should have been comforting, but it just amplified my frustration with myself. And then one afternoon, after I'd struggled to write a blog post, a feeble attempt to be funny through the fog of self-doubt and sadness, someone left a comment that said I was just recycling the same old jokes, and it was "getting old."

Now, on the spectrum of horrific things that people say when protected by the anonymity of the Internet, this is pretty far toward the "sugar and ponies" end of things. The amount of vitriol that I've had addressed to me over the years in grammatically problematic missives is both alarming and hilarious. If you are a woman on the Internet, this is par for the course—people who have never met you will say shocking things, mostly about your vagina, and occasionally, when they want to get really creepy, about your eyeballs.

If someone tells you that your jokes are getting old, it is basically the online equivalent of a gift basket, albeit one filled with culinarily specious treats like summer sausages and canned cheese (two things that should not be shelf-stable: meat and dairy). The most meaningful response it should elicit is an insincere thank-you and a witty retort. And yet when I read this accurate if insensitive comment, I promptly burst into tears. That comment hit far too close to a nerve.

"YOUR MOM IS GETTING OLD," I screamed at the computer, before scooting my keyboard out of the way, putting my head down on my desk, and wallowing in self-pity, in a way that Joan of Arc and Susan B. Anthony and Tina Turner and so many other heroic woman before me had not.

I tried to resume life as normal. We went on trips; I wandered around cities; I blogged. I felt like I'd stepped into someone else's life. I pretended I knew what I was doing. I pretended everything felt normal. After all, weren't things better now?

In January, Rand had actually taken a break with me in South Africa. We went back to Ireland in March and had a lovely time. We went to Australia in April and swam the Great Barrier Reef, which Rand had wanted to see since writing a report about it when he was nine. Then in the spring, I learned that a friend of mine from high school had died of brain cancer, leaving behind his wife and a son he'd never meet.

I felt guilty for being alive. I felt guilty for spending my days feeling terrible. I wanted to go back to how things were before all this had happened, but in this scenario Rand's promise to me didn't hold true: there was no cab that could take me back to how things were.

In the wake of loss and mired in depression, just before the one-year anniversary of my own surgery, Rand and I left for Paris for the second time in our lives. And for the first time, we actually made it there.

I'd heard from various other travelers, movies, and cartoons that Paris itself was a sort of chaotic nightmare, an overpriced tourist trap wrapped in a cliché. And that Parisians are universally horrible to everyone, but they reserve a special bit of loathing for Americans.

I was sufficiently petrified of this, and so I'd spent the last few months studying French, an endeavor at which I exhibited a level of such profound incompetence that even my seasoned tutor seemed taken aback. I'd nevertheless managed to keep a few important phrases in my head, which I will share now at no additional cost to you. A gratis lesson in Français, for which I ask nothing in return. Though I suppose if you did wish to thank me, the additional purchase of several more copies of this book might serve. It makes an excellent gift or a nominee for the National Book Award. But I digress.

French for the Wretched. Lesson 1:
> *"Je voudrais des macarons, s'il vous plaît."*
> *I would like some macarons, please.*
> *"J'ai chlamydia."*
> *I have chlamydia.*

In what will be both a defense and criticism of my French instructor, I will note that she only taught me that first phrase. I looked up the second one on my own.

For the record, I do not actually have chlamydia (despite what the captain of a rival high school debate team told everyone in the twelfth grade after we made out one time), but I imagined vivid scenarios in which falsely professing to have an STD might get me out of trouble in France. I would thwart pickpockets and mimes and an overly flirtatious Sarkozy by screaming it loudly, confusing them long enough for me to make my escape.

I also had a bunch of commonly used niceties in my wheelhouse, like *s'il vous plaît* and *merci beaucoup* and *désolé*, which means "I'm sorry."

As in, "Désolé, monsieur/madame, j'ai chlamydia."

None of this would prove to be even remotely necessary, but I've come to understand that we all do different things to better prepare ourselves for a trip. Rand likes to answer all his email, open up a fresh pair of contact lenses, and do extra exercises so his back will hurt less. I like to pack excess underwear and commit to memory the names of venereal diseases in the local language, a combination of actions that, I now realize, is somewhat alarming.

Paris triggered a special and unprecedented level of anxiety in me; this is noteworthy, as my calm is a normal person's panicked, and my panicked is a normal person's "OH, GOD, WHAT IS HAPPENING?"

Here is a short list of the things I expected to encounter in the city of light:

- dog shit (my friend Mindy had warned me that it peppered the city like an unholy seasoning),

- thieves, and
- a bunch of people who acted as though I had murdered them in another life.

But reality, once again, did not align with my expectations. I found none of what I had feared and no occasion to scream about STDs under the Arc de Triomphe. Instead, Paris would make good on every other promise made by the art nouveau movement and films starring Audrey Hepburn. There were broad streets lined with trees, down which elegantly dressed men and women strolled. There were red-painted lips and well-tailored suits, blooming flowers, ornate wrought-iron fences, and Metro signs designed by Hector Guimard. If you listened hard enough, you'd swear you could hear accordion music playing. Walking down the Champs-Élysées one warm afternoon, we actually did.

I pressed my nose against a bakery window and stared at the long cases inside, filled with macarons in a sea of colors, in flavors I couldn't have even dreamed of (not even during those dessert hallucinations that haunted me the week that I tried a paleo diet).

"Come back for me in three days," I whispered to Rand as he laughed.

Outwardly I smiled and tried to enjoy it all, while struggling with the sickening belief that it was wasted on me. Not just Paris, but all of it: the doting husband, the noncancerous brain, the endless pastries I shoved into my mouth with the subtlety of a squirrel finding a cache of nuts in midwinter.

Don't misunderstand me: I never thought I was deserving of the rich fairy tale that was my life. But it was indisputably mine. I now felt like those memories belonged to someone else.

That the surgery had somehow erased that previous iteration of Geraldine and I had taken her place.

I was an imposter in my own life.

I explained to a friend that it reminded me of an actor being replaced by another one halfway through a TV series. I've always gotten a huge kick out of the absurdity of it. No one seems to notice that Mom is now a sturdy blonde instead of a slim brunette, or that infants seem to age years over one summer hiatus. They just accept it. I've always assumed that inwardly, someone must be screaming.

During the filming of *Mad Men*, Don Draper's son was played by no fewer than four different actors, something that Rand and I took to joking about at length. Whenever the character got out of line, we'd scream things like, "Go to your room until we can replace you!" and "You don't hold a candle to Bobby #2!"

One full year after my surgery, that's how I felt. The elation of being alive was long gone, and I could only fixate on the fact that twelve months had passed, and I wasn't back to normal. It was as though Original Geraldine had been replaced with another one, and the rest of the cast failed to notice what was so glaringly obvious. And this new Geraldine was not someone I liked.

She was slower and quieter and had a frizzy patch of hair growing back through the scar tissue in her scalp. I know how self-pitying and vaguely psychotic this all sounds, but there was a strange, sick comfort in all of it as well. Hating myself made it much easier to deal with the guilt of being perfectly fine.

But getting lost gives you perspective. It always does. When you don't know where you are, the best thing to do is step back and try to make sense of things. For me, the turning point happened somewhere in the short walk between the Musée d'Orsay and the Louvre.

Art museums have always been a place of solace and contemplation for me. Other people meditate, or visit temples of worship, or take a hike in the woods. I wander the modern art wing. It requires less repentance and less cardio, and there's usually a café with cake.

That's where I find peace, being that particular breed of nerd who can stare at a seemingly nonsensical piece of art and clap her hands excitedly. Who can point out the influences of other masters in a painting or sculpture and be moved by all of it. I say this not to brag. It's just the sort of skill one acquires when still a virgin in her twenties.

I hadn't planned on visiting the d'Orsay. I overlooked it, as people so often do, failing to realize that whatever treasures were not in the Louvre were here. The d'Orsay is often overshadowed by its glitzy sibling, but Rand knew what it held. When I asked him which museum he wanted to tackle in Paris on his day off, he skipped over the perennial favorite and went straight for the Musée d'Orsay.

The Louvre, home to the *Mona Lisa*, would have been the obvious choice. But my husband is always wary of things that are too popular, too universally loved. He goes for dark horses and unconventionally beautiful things. I do not question him in this endeavor. I know precisely how I benefit from it.

The d'Orsay is vast and cavernous, an airplane hangar for humanity's brief moments of greatness. There is a massive central hall lined in mosaic tiles, with arched windows running down both sides. At one end, a massive clock hangs, just in case you should lose track of how jet lagged you are. Seeing it there, insisting that it was 2 p.m. when my heart and mind and the trail of spittle coming out of my mouth clearly insisted it was bedtime, felt like a microcosm of the last few months. The world was telling me one thing—that I was totally fine. I was insisting another—that I was now the sort of person who got mad at clocks.

The galleries shoot off this main hall, filled with anemic-looking Cézannes, pixelated Seurats, and enough Monets to fill a decade's worth of dental office calendars. Renoirs in which all the subjects looked soft and fuzzy, like those weird humanoid Muppets. There were Van Goghs, swirly and vibrant, each surrounded by a crowd of onlookers. The oft-told tale is that the doomed painter never sold a canvas in his lifetime and is now heralded as one of the greatest artists the world has ever seen. I suppose there is a lesson to be learned from that, but all I take away is heartache. Van Gogh died at thirty-seven.

In one gallery, I paused in front of a cluster of Toulouse-Lautrec's paintings of the Moulin Rouge. Even his most vibrant subjects—dancers and clowns—were gray-skinned and gaunt, looking as if they might at any minute die of consumption. I wonder if that was how Toulouse-Lautrec saw the world—fragile and sick. After having been plagued by illness all his life, he eventually succumbed to complications of alcoholism and syphilis at thirty-six.

It should have depressed me. Instead, I found odd comfort in the realization that nothing was eternal. I stared at the brush-strokes of geniuses who had died young and realized that even their works, no matter how much they were cared for, would eventually crumble and fade. But they still painted them because making something beautiful—even if it lasts for a second—is never futile.

Everything changes us. Brain surgeries, heartaches, divorces, bankruptcies, amputated ears, mental illness—it all helps to paint the picture of who we are at a precise moment in time. We are constantly adding layers of ourselves in brushstrokes big and small. The canvas is ever-evolving. Of course I wasn't the same person I was before my surgery. I wasn't the same person I was five minutes ago. None of us are.

That, I'd realize, was what I had to reckon with after surgery. Not trying to get back to who I was. That Geraldine was, for better or worse, gone. Instead, I needed to be okay with losing that part of myself. I needed to be comfortable with who I had become.

The next day, I went to the Louvre by myself. I'd anticipated something even grander than the Musée d'Orsay, even more majestic and lovely. Elaborate gilded frames and curving vines, all lit with a sepia-tinged glow, like Mucha paintings brought to life. Hallowed halls, as silent as an empty church.

The reality is less that and more like a college kegger. Lots of people shouting and taking selfies and touching the artwork because apparently it's not enough to look at it. You really need to *feel* Delacroix's brushstrokes to understand him.

The Louvre's layout does nothing to help mitigate its likeness to a drunken sex carnival. The architect clearly wanted to incorporate the classical into the modern while still remaining true to his roots as a sadist.

There is a wide cement courtyard, lined on three sides by the massive, U-shaped building, and the iconic glass pyramid sits alone in the middle. There is no shade in this courtyard, and if you neglected to get your ticket beforehand (which I did), this is where you will have to stand in line, hopefully briefly, baking in the midsummer Parisian sun (which, also, I did).

It was 10:30 a.m. on a Thursday, and so the line was relatively short. Within ten minutes I was inside the glass pyramid and took an elevator down one floor (only by going underground do you discover the pyramid is connected to the rest of the U-shaped building). This layout is ingenious, as it gives one relatively easy access to any wing of the museum, but also panic-inducing, as swarms of people head in different directions, usually while screaming in a plethora of languages.

It is okay to cry at this point. But know that it gets worse.

One level below the glass pyramid, you will become acutely aware that it acts like a magnifying glass above an anthill—its windows amplify and focus the searing June sun directly onto the crowds.

I breathed deeply. I needed to get out of there as soon as possible. I unfurled the map and decided I'd simply visit the works highlighted in the museum pamphlet. (It's probably the exact opposite of what Rick Steves would have done, but as I noted, he wears pleated-front pants across Europe, thus nullifying his opinion.)

The first item on my agenda was, of course, the *Mona Lisa*.

I'd seen her parodied countless times, seen reproductions of her image with its enigmatic smile and absent eyebrows—which may have been intentional or possibly a result of overzealous cleaning—time and again. I was delighted by the prospect of seeing the real thing.

I followed a series of signs that were posted all around the museum, bearing not only the painting's name but a small black-and-white reproduction of it as well, a rather considerate touch for those museum patrons unfamiliar with the Roman alphabet.

I wove through the Bacchanalia of the museum. There were people touching some of the statues; the nearby guards made no move to stop them—either they didn't notice, or perhaps they realized their efforts were Sisyphean and had wisely given up. Flashbulbs fired like heat lightning on ancient canvases, despite the many signs requesting that they be shut off.

After a twenty-minute trek, I turned a corner and found myself in the right gallery. At the end of it was the *Mona Lisa*, surrounded by a crowd of at least thirty people. I squeezed through, remembering the years I spent navigating concert crowds in my twenties (there was a brief, fleeting moment in my life when I may have been cool), and finally made it to the front.

There she was, smiling at me with her naked brow and odd little grin.

And there I was, utterly confused as to what the big deal was.

Other than a cautionary tale for why you should leave facial depilation in the hands of a professional, I didn't understand.

This is blasphemous, I know. She is a masterpiece, but I couldn't understand why. I stood there for a good while, waiting for one of the world's most famous paintings to resonate with me, and it didn't. I gave it a fair chance. I held my ground, near the front, while my fellow museum patrons jostled next to me with all the subtlety and grace of a mob of Black Friday shoppers.

I'd heard that the painting was smaller than most people expect it to be, so I was prepared for that, but not for how underwhelmed I'd be. I've heard time and again that some things lose their magic when you see them in person, but I've found that in my travels, the opposite is more often true. Believe me when I tell you that the Pantheon will render you speechless. And that Jay-Z, whom I once saw in New York before he disappeared in a puff of lavender smoke, is an Adonis in a white suit.

But the *Mona Lisa* did not speak to me. She didn't move me to tears, reminding me of my own lonely and defiant years, like Degas's *Little Dancer Aged Fourteen*, or leave me elated and speechless, like Seurat's *The Models*. She didn't even give me a hint as to why she was smiling. Instead, I found myself disappointed with one of the most famous paintings in the world.

And once again, there I was, weirdly comforted by it.

Because if Leonardo da Vinci disappoints you, there's a good chance that you have unreasonable expectations of everything, including yourself.

Perhaps not everyone needs to agree that something is amazing for it to be so. Maybe it is hard to smile without eyebrows or an intact skull. We do it anyway, and maybe that is enough. Maybe I needed more time. Or maybe I was different now, and maybe everything was changed, but Rand still thought I was a masterpiece and I needed to be as accepting of that as I was of these mad fools competing to take a blurry selfie with *Mona*.

Not everyone will see our greatness. We might not even see it. That doesn't mean it isn't there.

By the time Rand found me back at the hotel, I was lying on our bed, eating macarons and humming what I thought was the French national anthem, but may have actually been the theme to *The A-Team* (to those who judge me for this blunder:

guess which tune will remain stuck in your head for the rest of the day).

"How was the Louvre?" he asked.

"Ugh. A madhouse. I spent half an hour looking for the painting of the two naked chicks where one is pinching the other's nipple."

I should explain. After I'd found the *Mona Lisa*, I'd circled the Louvre for a good part of the afternoon looking for the works mentioned in the museum map. One painting included therein, *Gabrielle d'Estrées and One of Her Sisters*, artist unknown, features the eponymous Gabrielle sitting naked in a bath with her sister—because apparently that's what French aristocracy did in the 1500s. And while they look rather prim and proper for two grown women sharing a tub, the sister is reaching over and pinching Gabrielle's nipple—supposedly a nod to her fertility, as Gabrielle was pregnant with Henry IV's son. I bet Thanksgiving, if it had existed at the time, would have been *crazy* at their house.

Rand laughed. I lay on the bed, eating macarons that I had ordered from a patisserie with such pitiful determination that the woman behind the counter gave me a free one, thereby forever cementing this valuable lesson: ineptitude pays.

I nibbled on the spoils of my pathetic effort as I relayed the afternoon to Rand. I told him a remarkable truth about the Louvre: the galleries are numbered, but in each wing of the museum, the counting starts anew. There are several galleries numbered 14 or 15 or 16. So all the signs might be telling you that you are in the right place, but you know that they're wrong.

And just when you start to think you are losing your mind, you find some empty corner of the museum that you have just to yourself, and you see something beautiful—a painting you've loved for years, the poster of which was once hanging in your college studio—and you find yourself thinking that it's okay. You will never find the exit, but that was all okay.

Rand smiled, arms crossed as he leaned against a desk, listening to every word.

"Do you want some steak frites?" he asked when I'd finished my rant.

Yes. Yes. A thousand times yes. I'd have shouted this reply had my mouth not been full of salted caramel meringue. But I didn't need to verbalize it—Rand knew the answer, anyway. In a world where nothing is constant and nothing lasts, it is nice to know that some things are etched in stone—time or brain surgery or jet lag cannot alter them. I would always get lost. And I would always make it back. Sometimes I'd have to lose a sweater, or a piece of luggage, or a part of my skull, but I would make it back. Maybe I had changed. And maybe it didn't matter. He was still there to listen to my misadventures, to feed me and hold me close.

I don't know how many years we have left, he and I. I don't know if we'll bow out early like Messrs. Toulouse-Lautrec and Van Gogh, or if we'll be around long enough to watch the other's hair grow gray. I just know that in a world where nothing is constant, when I can't even be sure of myself, this one thing endures.

The truth is, roads move only in one direction, no matter how hard you try or how desperately you scream at traffic. You take a deep breath, and you accept that you are going somewhere new. You will get used to this new place, to your new reflection, to the dent in your head. If you are very, very lucky, you will find a familiar face when you get there. He will smile at you as he always has and ask if you want to get steak frites.

You realize that you are exactly where you are supposed to be. It just looks a little different than you'd imagined.

15

MUNICH—LAND OF SAUSAGES AND EPIPHANIES

TRAVEL DIDN'T JUST HELP ME make sense of myself. It helped me make sense of those closest to me. While narrowly avoiding strip searches with my mother or trekking across London to find that damn clock that my father loved, I started, in some small way, to understand them better.

But my older brother Edward has always been another matter. I could go to the ends of the earth and things between us would remain rocky, as they have been all my life. After years of fighting this notion, I've just come to accept it. You don't need to like a person or a place to have it be integral to who you are.

It's like your butthole. Do you like your butthole? Probably not. Some of you might, and that's cool. It's good to like yourself. But odds are it's probably not your favorite body part. Still, you're grateful for it, because it is *your* butthole and you don't know where you'd be without it.

This is how I've come to regard Edward. He's a butthole. But he's *my* butthole.

At some point, I suspect he had to accept the fact that he and I were stuck with each other. But I never had this realization; from my perspective, Edward and I never met for the first time. The concept is utterly absurd, like meeting my own limbs or my reflection in the mirror. Edward has simply always been, as long as I have existed.

My mother, though, remembers our first encounter well and delights in retelling it.

"He wanted to throw you in the trash," Mom explains. "But I told him we couldn't, because you'd cry."

My brother, ever the problem solver, pressed on.

"So then he suggested we take you back to the hospital. But I told him we couldn't do that because you'd be all alone and hungry and cold. So he said, 'Fine. Fine, I guess we can keep her.' Isn't that so sweet?"

Those were Edward's first impressions of me. But I have no first impressions of him. He's just always been a part of my life, as permanently a part of me as a freckle on my arm. Getting rid of either would leave a scar, an indelible reminder that a part of me was now gone.

He is the reason why my right arm doesn't bend properly, a result of a break sustained in the summer of 1987. We were both on our bikes. Blame for this incident remains hotly debated to this day. He was the impetus for dying my hair blue when I was thirteen. And he is why my knowledge of science fiction is as uselessly vast as it is.

My friend Nora relayed something her mother told her, which I always found lovely and completely inapplicable to my relationship with Edward: "No one will know you like your sibling does."

In my life, I've found this variant to be more accurate: "No one will know *how to make you seriously consider fratricide* like your sibling does."

Growing up in my family was a singular experience, one with a long legacy, whether it be in therapy bills or ill-advised tattoos or that haircut I got sophomore year of college that can best be described as a buzz cut with bangs. My family, never big on taking photos when my hair looks good, has documented it very well.

I don't think it would be fair to describe the residual effects of growing up in my family as Stockholm syndrome, for I have been to Stockholm and it is a very lovely and sane place. Perhaps a better term would be "that weird part of town usually situated next to the airport" syndrome. (Due to financial constraints and bad judgment, that's where my family almost always resides.) But that's a bit wordy.

I always assumed he and I would be better friends. We'd be impervious to fighting, tied together by inside jokes, with the exact same shade of hair color and the sort of unbreakable bond that comes from being in a foxhole together.

I was recently visiting him in L.A., and I misread the time of my flight back to Seattle. I was in a panic, and Edward, in order to calm me down, decided to escalate the situation.

"You know what happens if you miss this flight?"

"I know, I know. I can just get on the next one."

"Nope. This is the last flight to Seattle, ever. You miss it, and the world will end."

"Goddamn it, Edward."

"Seriously, we're going to round this corner and there are going to be overturned cars and fires everywhere and people screaming. It's the end of days."

And rather than panic, I just started laughing, which I suspected was his plan all along. Sometimes, he knows me better than I know myself.

But it's hard to know when he's tormenting me for my own good and when he's just tormenting me. When asked about him, the best I can come up with is this: We are close. But we don't get along.

Sometimes, after a particularly nasty fight with Edward, I will tell Rand that I'm done.

"I'm never seeing him again," I'll say.

"Okay," Rand replies, obligingly.

"*I mean it.*"

"Alright."

"NEVER EVER AGAIN."

"Sounds good."

What my husband never lets on is precisely how empty he knows my proclamations are. It is the vow of every ignored little sister and overlooked younger brother. I have sworn time and again that I was done with Edward. That he'd infuriated me or made me cry or tweeted that I was the best big sister ever *even though he is four years older than me* for the last time.

I don't need him.

I try to convince Rand of this. I try to convince Edward. I try to convince myself. It's all lies.

I spent the first fourteen years of my life following him around, hoping for some small sign of approval or friendship. I was the prototypical annoying little sister: always around, bursting through every private moment (the day I learned to pick the bathroom lock was a grand one), and desperately needy.

Share all the attention and love and Halloween candy you will ever receive with me. And love me, even when I kick you in the testicles.

Honestly, is that so much to ask?

I remember every instance of kindness he's ever shown me. I remember the half hug he gave me when I broke my arm that fateful summer—a quick, sideways squeeze and a peck on the top of my head that lasted only a split second. Was it an admission of guilt? I can't say. I only know that it proved more effective than codeine. I barely remember the nausea that followed the ingestion of those painkillers. But I remember that hug and have for more than a quarter of a century.

It was the same hug he'd give me seven years later, when he left for college. His friend Chris and I dropped him off at the airport and drove back home in silence, each of us trying not to cry, unsure of who would antagonize us now.

I would argue that Edward and I are entirely dissimilar, but there are strange overlaps. Every now and then I will start to wax—not poetic but indignant—about some topic. A long, rambling monologue that usually results in my voice becoming louder and more high-pitched as I fight with some invisible adversary.

Rand usually says nothing during these soliloquies (though he will sometimes nudge me and whisper, "Baby, you're shouting") and lets me work through whatever it is I'm frustrated about.

And then he will look at me and say, "All done, Edward?"

This reply would have annoyed a younger me to no end. But after all these years I realize the truth in it. Oddly, both my and

Edward's spouses can see the similarities that we once refused to acknowledge.

Val, my brother's wife, has said this time and again, whenever Edward and I have a similar reaction or express a similar preference about something.

"You guys are so alike. You don't see it, but you are."

She's wrong: sometimes I do see it. Sometimes. In our penchant for pumpkin-flavored desserts and 1980s action movies. In the sad realization that neither of us inherited our mother's metabolism. In a deep and profound disdain for the actor Zach Braff. (I suspect it even stems from the same reason: Braff and my brother look alarmingly alike. The pouty lips, the floppy hair, the Gen X ennui. Really, the only fundamental difference is that Zach Braff has an estimated net worth of $22 million, and Edward . . . has a vast collection of Transformers.)

My brother has spent the past twenty years waiting for his break in Hollywood. Southern California is where he lives, where he got married, where his son was born. (Xander came on the scene just a few weeks after my brain surgery. The timing was such that I wouldn't meet him until several months later, at Thanksgiving. I ran for the door when they arrived, and Edward held the carrier away from me. "Two dollars," he said. "For two dollars, you can look at my son. Otherwise, nothing.")

He doesn't tell me about his projects. I usually find out about them by checking his IMDB page. If I am lucky, I'll find one of his films on TV. Most of them are low-budget horror or sci-fi films. I have seen him be murdered by a homicidal clown, be possessed by some sort of evil rock from space that made him a psychic, and get vaporized by an alien. Giant robots feature prominently in my brother's theatrical canon.

He writes a lot of scripts and screenplays as well (I have tried and failed to understand the difference). They are occasionally made into films, and he might get one of the dozen parts that he wrote with himself in mind.

The finished product will undergo a large number of re-writes or edits. The antagonist will change from an oppressive postapocalyptic social structure to a two-headed shark. ("Is it a metaphor?" I will gently ask. "No," he'll reply. "It's a fucking two-headed shark.") The independent, fight-the-establishment matriarch will now be played by Carmen Electra in a bikini.

But if I pay close attention, I can see little glimpses—a joke or a brilliant line—that are truly Edward's.

Our real lives follow that same pattern. I've concluded that this person—this cranky, critical man—is not authentic but the result of rewrites and edits. Instead, it's the times when we laugh together—when no one gets our joke but us—that I see the real him.

But those moments are so few and far between, I sometimes doubt it.

Los Angeles doesn't remind me of my brother. I know it's his home, but there is nothing familiar about L.A. to me, though nearly everything about Edward is. I don't understand the end-less sunshine or the noisy wealth or the tendency of so many of its residents to cut off perfectly good noses. It all seems wasteful.

The Edward that I grew up with, the chubby kid who I once saw eat an entire half of a pumpkin pie in a single sitting, holding the massive hemisphere like a slice of watermelon in his hands, does not fit in that world. It is home to a new articulation of him, one that spends hours at the gym and consumes only lean protein.

It is not that glittering metropolis, the one where he's lived for twenty years, that reminds me of him, but rather the Bavarian city of Munich. It's where he was born, so long ago that his birth certificate reads "West Germany." It is in that place, where we never lived together, that he becomes inescapable.

Rand and I go to Munich nearly every year. He's often invited to conferences there, and we use the trip as an excuse to see my dad, who lives about an hour away. Without fail we spend a few days in the city before going to visit him.

Munich has become a staple in our travel itineraries, a port of call that we always return to. But even after so many visits, I can't tell if I like it or not. It's easy to dismiss it as too cold and formal. A bit too sterile, a bit too rigid. On some trips, I make an extra effort to seek out something fun. I take the subway or bus to some random museum, spend the morning looking at sculptures in the Glyptothek or a hangar full of planes in the Deutsches Museum.

Yet the harder I work to enjoy the city, the less fun I have. It's only when I roam around expecting nothing that I discover some magical park or museum I didn't know about, some doughnut stand or bierhalle that had escaped my notice on earlier trips.

I'm sure there's a lesson there.

I remember my grandmother telling me how, when Edward was an infant, my father would get up with him at whatever ungodly hour it was and carry him to his workshop. There, he'd balance Edward with one hand and work on a miniature remote control plane with the other, until my brother fell asleep again or Mom got up.

I realize the improbability of the story, but I like it just the same. My father has always been a fanatic for cars and planes.

His creations were always precise and meticulous—German engineering at its finest.

In many of the photos from my brother's early childhood, Edward is wandering around my parents' Munich apartment, diaper-clad, wielding a red biplane Dad built for him, his name written across the wingspan in big black letters: EDWARD.

It was labeled for no reason other than to do it. Back then there would have been no confusion as to its owner. There was no one with whom he had to share.

A few short years later Mom would leave for America to have me, and in doing so, everything changed for Edward overnight: his home country, the languages spoken around him, his status as an only child, his relationship with our father.

I know it's not my fault, but when I arrived, everything was different. He wasn't even four. Sometimes I can't blame him for blaming me.

Munich would become my brother's one childhood home that was his alone. In the years since, I've been there more than he has.

In the spring of 2013, not long after my nephew Xander was born and the dent in my head felt mostly healed, Edward wrote to me to say that he and Val were going to Germany to introduce their son to Dad. Did we want to join them?

I'd waited thirty years to be included in my brother's plans. Yes, I said. Yes, we'll be there.

We got into town a few days before he did, and so I was there when Val walked up, carrying Xander. I saw the look on my dad's face when he saw his grandson for the first time, the flicker of delight interrupting his scowl.

It lasted a good three seconds, which is an eternity in my dad's world.

"Why the hell isn't that kid walking on his own?" he asked.

"Dad, he's nine months old."

My father rolled his eyes. My brother had given him the greatest gift he could ask for: an entirely new generation with whom to be exasperated.

For several days, we resided under the same roof with relatively few casualties (a rather unprecedented achievement). The village where my dad lives is incredibly small and quiet, surrounded entirely by farmlands. In the springtime, the air is heavy with the scent of fresh-cut grass and manure.

It is one of the most boring places on earth, in a pleasant way.

"I have something for him," my father announced one morning, gesturing to Xander, before heading downstairs to his workshop (it's been years since he lived in the small Munich apartment that my brother had called home, but Dad has always had a place where he builds his planes).

He returned with a tiny pair of leather sandals and placed them on the ground in front of my nephew. Blue and strappy, the toddler equivalent of Birkenstocks. On the leather foot bed was stamped the words "West Germany."

My dad, the shockingly unsentimental man who disdained clutter, who kept absolutely nothing, had held on to a pair of my brother's baby shoes for thirty-five years. I wondered if he'd found them after my mom had left for America with Edward, hidden in some drawer. How long he held on to them before he realized that his son had outgrown them. That my mother wasn't coming back. Was it a conscious decision to keep them until some grandchild could wear them? Or was he simply unable to throw them out?

I never got an answer. I can't ask my dad things like that, any more than I can ask Edward why his interpretation of the role of big brother is always to be my chief tormentor. These are things that will remain forever undiscussed. The Italian side is the one that has no secrets, that leaves no thought unspoken, no grievance unscreamed. But there are conversations between my brother and father and me that will never take place, things that remain tucked away in the back of closets for thirty years. I've come to terms with this, embraced the idea that you need to occasionally accept things as they are.

Munich will always feel cold; Rome will always be chaotic; Los Angeles will always wear its superficiality like a badge of honor. It's just how it is.

Rand and I were scheduled to go home before Edward and Val, and on our last day together, my brother and his family drove into downtown Munich with us.

We walked through the central square—a wide promenade lined with shops and the occasional ancient church or museum. Shoppers and tourists moved through it with surprising efficiency, occasionally blocked by throngs of Italian teenagers on school trips. Looming over all of it was the Rathaus—the large, ominous city hall, lined with spires, with an enormous glockenspiel at the center.

Edward held Xander one-armed, and it was as we walked through this bustling part of downtown that he realized his son's diaper had leaked. My brother had a wide splotch of baby urine on the front of his shirt.

He laughed, unconcerned. My brother, who I'd seen lose his shit over broken pencil lead, was laughing about a urine-stained shirt.

Those of us who are childless, who have watched our siblings make that miraculous and mucusy transformation into parents, are usually taken aback by behavior like this. I've found the best solution is to lean in and gently take your brother's or sister's face in your hands. From this vantage point, it's hard not to see the kid they were. There are crow's feet around their eyes, but the eyes are nevertheless the same. After a few quiet moments of beautiful introspection with your face awkwardly close to theirs, yell "YOU ARE A POD PERSON" at the top of your lungs without warning. This is a really good tactic when trying to accept the fact that you can know someone for an eternity and not have the faintest clue as to who they are.

Also, pod people *hate* that sort of thing.

"Uh . . . we need a bathroom," my pod-brother said, emitting a faint laugh as he gestured to the front of his urine-stained shirt.

Given the ubiquity of beer in Munich, you'd assume that toilets would be easy to find. But the city's engineers either had massive bladders or a dark sense of humor, because public bathrooms are few and far between. I'd visited the city enough times to know exactly where one was: just inside the interior courtyard of the Rathaus, on the right, you can find a small bank of toilets. For the relatively low price of half a euro (which, when you have a bladder or shirtfront that is full of urine, seems like a good deal), you can partake in using an incredibly clean and well-stocked bathroom.

There, my brother took his son in to change his diaper.

And it was there, just outside the bathroom, that my brother did something that caused an immediate flashback to my own childhood. He grabbed Xander's tiny fist and gently throttled his face with it, making "pssht-pssht" noises while yelling, "STOP HITTING YOURSELF. STOP HITTING YOURSELF."

"Edward," I snapped, remembering the many afternoons he'd inflicted the same misery upon me, "stop it."

"I'm not doing anything." He continued faux-punching his son.

"Edward," I said again, my voice echoing up the walls of the Rathaus courtyard, "STOP PUNCHING YOUR BABY."

"He's my baby. I can punch him if I want to."

"STOP IT."

"He likes it."

"HE DOES NOT."

"Yes, he does. Watch."

Edward pretended to punch Xander, making slow-motion jabs to his face and cheeks accompanied by a *pssht-pssht* sound.

And, god help me, the kid loved it. He laughed, waving his arms up and down maniacally. I wondered if maybe I hadn't spent an entire childhood unloved. If maybe the problem had simply been that I wasn't the right audience.

Maybe I was always asking the wrong thing of him. I wanted him to love me and look out for me. That's not my brother. But if you need someone to criticize your haircut ("You look like an angler fish," he once said of my asymmetrical bob) and question every single decision you've ever made ("That's what you're wearing?" he asked me on my wedding day), then my brother is your man.

I just wasn't playing to his strengths. I wasn't seeing him for what he was, in the same way I didn't see Munich for what it was. On past trips, I'd spent hours looking for shops or cafés and found the city wanting. But had I been searching for giant heart-shaped gingerbread cookies that read "ICH LIEBE DICH" (which, to my horrified delight, is how you say "I love you" in German) or a salad made entirely of sausage, I'd have been in the right place. I was just looking for the wrong thing.

Later, I walked us to a series of cheap shops along the promenade in search of a new shirt for Edward. He didn't end up buying one.

"It's just baby pee," he said, using the kind of logic that makes sense to new parents but is somewhat horrifying to those of us who are childless.

We led them up to a small restaurant we knew of, just around the corner from the Viktualienmarkt, less crazy than the Augustiner Bierhalle that dotted the city. It was dark and cozy and warm, smelling of beer and fresh bread. We ate schnitzel and sausage and spaetzle, all the gloriously unhealthy food groups that my brother avoided in L.A.

And then, on a sidewalk in Munich, under a gray sky, we said goodbye, Edward giving me a quick half hug, as he always did. They headed back to our dad's house. We were heading home.

I was quiet on our drive out of the city.

"You okay?" Rand asked.

I shrugged.

"We had a nice time," he said, and it was true, but I remained disappointed.

"It's just . . . I knew exactly where a bathroom was when he needed one. I knew where he could get a new cheap shirt, and where to eat, and I feel like he barely noticed."

The truth was out: I'd just wanted to impress him.

Look, I wanted to say. *Look at how much I know about this city that I don't really like that much but still love, just because it reminds me of you. Look.*

"He just doesn't say stuff like that," Rand said. "I think sometimes you expect too much of people."

I nodded.

A few hours later, we received an email from my brother. The last line was this:

"Good seeing you guys. Miss you already."

I stared at it, knowing that I would hang on to it for far too long. Like the memory of the hug from the summer I broke my arm. Like the tiny pair of leather shoes in my father's home, the ones that their owner had long since outgrown.

If I were to venture into my brother's creative realm and write the screenplay of my life, I have to acknowledge two things. The first is that there would be scenes shot in Munich, a city that I don't necessarily like but am inexorably tied to.

The second is that the part of Edward would be essential to the story; it'd be impossible to leave him on the cutting room floor. Obnoxious and loud, brash and brilliantly funny. My vulnerable villain, the antagonizer I can't live without. It's a role my brother was born to play.

I'd cast Zach Braff in the part.

16

WHERE THERE'S A FIAT,
THERE'S A WAY

BELIEVE IT OR NOT, I didn't realize that my journeys over
the past seven years were going to lead to all this introspection
about and understanding of the people closest to me. At the
start, my plan was to eat a lot of cake and do my best not to
cause any international incidents. The weaving together of disparate places and people into a wonderful tapestry of memories
large enough to cover the planet was just a delightful side effect.

Rand kept true to his promise of trying to find a work-life
balance, and I kept true to my promise of eating frosting for
dinner at least once a month. And almost everything in my life
seemed to fit together.

But there were some pieces that remained separate, as much
as I tried. The love of my life, Rand, and the loves of my childhood, my nonno and nonna, had missed meeting one another
by a span of a few months. I could travel the world again and

again, and I'd never be able to change this immutable fact. That every boy who ever broke my heart had the privilege of meeting them, of being the subject of countless stories I told my grandmother while sitting next to her on the couch as she intently listened. Every single one, right up until the one that really mattered, got to know them.

I adored my grandparents, which, in hindsight, is kind of a terrible idea.

It's like buying an eight-year-old a hamster, which we, as a society, universally do. I think there's some sort of national register for it: you turn eight and someone hands you a hamster.

And then you get really attached to the hamster and make long-term plans about taking the hamster to college, and all of it is just awful because—and my sincerest apologies if this is news—your lives are going to overlap for a year or two at most.

But it happens anyway, and I suppose it's wonderful that it does, because cedar shavings and odd-smelling food pellets and those cute furry cheeks stuffed with sunflower seeds teach you about life and death.

While my love for my grandparents far exceeded any affection I felt for my hamster (Anastasia Elizabeth Cottonball DeRuiter, RIP), there was something similarly tragic and wonderful about loving them. These were people who were already old *before I was even born*.

Had I had any sense in my tiny head, I'd have looked at my grandparents and said, "Look, you guys are just great, but I can tell that this isn't going to be a long-term thing, and you're just going to break my heart." And then I'd have nobly walked back into my playroom, promptly destroying any gravitas I may have earned by harvesting and ingesting my own boogers.

But like most children, I was illogical and not really forward-thinking, and so I delighted in my grandparents. In nearly every photo from my childhood, I'm clinging to one or the other of them. When they died toward the end of my junior year of college, I was ill-prepared for their deaths.

My grandmother passed away in the spring of 2001, and my grandfather was gone not long after. A few days after his funeral, I was unceremoniously dumped by a boyfriend who told me that it wasn't all that fun to date someone who was "sad all the time." When I learned that I couldn't lure him back with hysterical crying, I went to Italy for a month, because it's always a good idea to spread your drunken grief across two continents, if you can. What few memories I do have from that period are tinged pink from a 2000 Montepulciano d'Abruzzo, of which, based on conservative estimates, I drank approximately forty-three gallons (I think, anyway. Most of it was in liters).

Nearly all the people I've ever known who have lost someone close to them have told me that there are certain spots in the world where they've always expected to bump into them. That they couldn't shake the feeling that they'd find them in the corner of a favorite bar or sitting on a bench in the park, or that they might walk through the front door of their house any minute. It's not that we don't realize the people we care about are gone— it's just a weird little trick that our brains play on us that causes us to tie people to places on Earth long after they've left it. Even the terminology that we use tends to support this crazed notion. "We lost her last year" implies that if we look hard enough, we'll find her. She isn't gone. She's just been temporarily misplaced.

During that messy summer after they died, I visited my grandparents' village for the first time. And though my head knew that the effort was fruitless, my heart kept expecting to turn a corner to find the two of them sitting down, playing cards or eating pasta or having espresso. In my impossible day-dream they were not as they'd been in their final years, but younger and healthier, the vibrant grandparents I remembered from when I was small, when America was new to them and the world was new to me.

They weren't there, of course. Instead, I just walked the tiny village streets where they once had, and, if such a thing was possible, felt their absence even more acutely.

In early September 2001, I went back home. Three months after that messy summer ended, I caught a bus in the middle of the night on my way back from a concert. The love of my life happened to be on it. And so the three most important people in my life missed meeting each other by a matter of months.

I couldn't take Rand to meet my grandparents. But I could take him to their village, on a mountaintop not far from Naples. It took me forever to get there. It always does.

In the spring of 2014, a year after we'd met my brother in Munich, Rand's work called him back to that city again. A week later he had a conference in Boston, and Rand suggested we spend the days in between in Italy. We flew into Naples, thrown from the order and cleanliness of Germany into the vibrant chaos of southern Italy. Lines of laundry left outside to dry fluttered in the wind, the unofficial flag of the south. In just a few short hours, I went from a city that belonged to my brother to one that belonged to my grandparents. I hadn't been there since my trip with Kati.

The sun was setting as we picked up our rental car—a lumbering beast of a Peugeot—the only automatic car in the entire fleet. We stared at it, disbelieving. It was mid-sized by American standards and positively massive by Italian ones. The roads in this part of the world felt like carnival rides: unstable and hastily thrown together, leaving you with the feeling that you were at any moment going to totter off some edge, head first. We were plowing down them in what felt like a parade float.

We drove, the sun casting Naples in a yellow-orange glow, Vesuvius looming large in the background, already turning indigo in the receding light.

I wasn't worried about Rand navigating southern Italian roads, even in the dark—he could make sense of the madness. It was one of the reasons why our relationship worked and why my family loved him so much. Throw Rand in the middle of crazy, and he will coast through it.

The GPS on his phone led us from the highway to the hills on the horizon. We passed a sign that pointed to a dusty road off to the right.

"Guardia dei Lombardi"—the village where my grandmother was from. I excitedly pointed it out to Rand, but it was already far behind us, and he was too busy trying to follow the prompts of Google Maps to take note.

"I'm sorry," he said, "Did you need me to turn back there?"

"No, no," I said. "Just pointing it out."

When I was little, I had no frame of reference for what this part of the world looked like. My grandfather would occasionally head back to Italy, and I'd stand on tiptoe and peek inside his luggage as he packed. It was always fascinating to me—his wildly printed ties, his bright shirts, all neatly folded inside a green, hard-sided suitcase bearing the misnomer "American Tourister."

"Nonno, dove vai?" I'd ask. *Where are you going?*

"In Campania," he'd reply. He was referring to the name of the region that could be found just below Italy's shin where my grandparents were from. But as a child, I didn't know that Campania, and confused it with the similar-sounding word *campagna*, which means "countryside." And so I had a misguided vision of my grandfather trekking across fields and streams in his suit and tie.

Which, looking at the landscape, wasn't *that* far off. The reality was even rockier and dustier than I had envisioned, the villages seeming to come straight from the earth, carved from the surrounding rocks. The stone houses were laid in rows, one next to the other, each sharing a wall with its neighbor. The flat façades formed long corridors that cut through the village like a maze.

When I was little, I knew none of this. Not that my grandfather's village was in the mountains, or that my grandmother's was nearby. I knew only that their country was boot-shaped and it stuck out oddly into the sea, a permanently misplaced step into the water.

Later, as I grew older, the details of my family history would be filled in. Nonna was from Guardia dei Lombardi—Guardia for short. Nonno was from the neighboring village of Frigento. Back then it was (and frankly, still sort of is) taboo to marry someone from your own village. This makes sense—when your town consists of only a few thousand or even a few hundred people, you need to wade a little further out of the gene pool.

So you can imagine the reception my grandfather received when he returned home with my grandmother, and she had her five pretty younger sisters in tow. Overnight, my grandfather increased the female population of the village by 0.25 percent; because they were from a neighboring village, they were entirely eligible. I think part of the reason so many people in Frigento still remember my grandfather, even today, is that they owe their very existence to him.

He was the life of the party, but my grandmother was the heart of everything. She pulled everyone toward her, not by demanding attention but by giving it. She would ask if we were hungry and, regardless of the response, would spend long hours in the kitchen, emerging with massive pots of pasta or pizzas the size of coffee tables. She would sit, quietly, listening intently to whatever anyone had to say, distracted only on occasion by her own sadness. My mother said that it stemmed from the death of my nonna's infant daughter, for whom I was named. The fact that I was the second Geraldina to come along meant that my role in her life was already written: a recipient of all that deeply stowed love, a tiny counterweight to her decades of grief, a demander of candies.

She was small in stature, but because my entire world seemed to move around her, it escaped my notice. In the scope of my life, she was a giant. She made a room warmer just by being in it. She made me believe I had stories worth telling.

The pin-straight hair and cheekbones I inherited from her, along with an affinity for oversized cardigans and a disdain for wearing socks to bed, despite my freezing toes.

I adored her. As I got older, it became an increasing source of anxiety for me. She grew frailer; I knew it wouldn't last.

✳ ✳ ✳

WATCHING RAND DRIVE TOWARD where the map indicated, something felt not quite right. The distance felt too long, but not because I remembered the drive. I'd been there only twice before: once right after my grandparents passed away and again a few years later with my mother. I'd stayed there only a matter of hours and days, respectively, and even my most recent jaunt out there was nearly a decade ago.

No, the reason the road felt wrong was this: I knew my grandfather quite well, and I couldn't imagine him going all this way, even for a wife.

I don't mean to be unromantic, but I'm a realist. A fifteen-minute drive is roughly ten minutes longer than my grandfather would have been willing to go to meet the woman he'd be married to for more than sixty years. He spent time on his hair. Not on chivalry.

We drove on, nothing looking familiar, nothing feeling right. The light was nearly gone now, the mountains dark shadows against the indigo sky.

A few minutes later, we were standing in a stone square at the center of which was a large fountain. Lovely and serene, softly lit, the sort of place that had and would continue to look the same for centuries. There was just one problem: it was not the right mountaintop village.

I explained this to Rand.

"But this is where Google Maps said it was," he protested.

"This is southern Italy," I said, waving my hands in the middle of the square like a local. "Nothing is where *anything* says it is."

I know I am in my mother's homeland when the civil engineering is so nonsensical that not even the most powerful entities on the planet, aided by satellite technology, can make sense of it. Google definitely knows what style of underwear I prefer (full-coverage cotton granny panties, because we're almost at the end of the book, and let's be honest, there really isn't any mystery left at this point), but once you get south of Bologna, you're on your own.

Rand and I squinted at the map on his phone—we were in Villa Maina. I followed the road back with my finger, tracing a squiggle on the screen of the phone until I saw it: Frigento.

"There," I said, pointing to a dot at the summit of one of the peaks.

We retraced our drive, and once again found the sign for Guardia dei Lombardi that I'd pointed out before. From this new angle of approach, we could see another sign, small and somewhat hidden, pointing up in the same direction.

"Frigento," it read.

"You have *got* to be kidding me," Rand said. "How the hell were we supposed to see that?"

"Shhhh," I said, gently stroking his hair. "It's Italy. It's not supposed to make sense."

When we stepped out of the car for the second time that night, I knew we were in the right place. I'd barely spent any time there, but on some fundamental genetic level, I was able to decipher something that even satellite navigation could not: that everything started here.

There was little greenery—only stone, which made up the houses, the streets, the courtyards. There were gardens, but they were hidden from view, nestled behind each house in adjacent rows. The streets looked as though they should have been open to pedestrians only, but the concept of prohibiting a car from going somewhere doesn't really exist in Italy. Piazzas, sidewalks, staircases—where there's a Fiat, there's a way.

The roads all wound up in the same direction, toward the summit of the little mountain. It was chilly and dead quiet, and surprisingly well lit. Orange light spilled out from dozens of lampposts, casting everything in a coral glow.

Somewhere, wood was burning, and the warm, charred scent caught on the air, mixed with the faint fragrance of the first flowers of spring.

Even if I had never seen it before, I'd have known this was the right place.

We stayed in a tiny bed and breakfast on the bottom floor of one of the stone houses, a dark cave of a room, absurdly affordable if a bit chilly. We were meeting my family the next day, Sunday, for *pranzo*—the midday meal in Italy, usually the largest one of the day, and on Sundays a several-hours-long undertaking. Tomorrow's *pranzo* would be at my aunt Rosamaria's house. She was my mother's first cousin; her mother, the only one of my grandmother's five lovely sisters that was still on this earth, lived in the house adjacent to her. We'd be joined by Rosamaria's husband and brother (both named Gino), as well as my Uncle Enzo, his wife, Antonietta, and my cousin, Valeria, who were driving three hours just to see us.

The next morning we woke early, heard the soft chirp of birds and the distant sound of church bells, and wandered through the village, passing the occasional widow, clad head to toe in black, on her way to mass.

We wished the women "Buongiorno," a greeting that they returned, seemingly surprised we addressed them in Italian. I didn't know any of them, but their faces as they passed weren't

entirely foreign to me. I'd seen bits and pieces of them before—
an eyebrow here, a dimple there, their faces assembled from the
same molds as those of my family had been. I assumed that I
was exempt from this (I've always favored my father, with his
formidable nose and mustache). But more than once over the
next few days, when I mentioned who my family was, people
would nod and say, "Yes, I can see it in your face." And I'd sup-
press the desire to kiss them, full on the lips.

We wandered through town, stopped at a little fruit stand,
and bought a few tangerines and a handful of cherry toma-
toes that we ate by the side of the road, watching people pass. I
would have led us to my Aunt Rosamaria's house, but I wasn't
sure which one it was.

"The door is green," I offered to Rand, which wasn't at all
helpful. So instead we sat on a low stone wall, and I assumed
that the answer would come to me. It did, in the form of a
white-haired gentleman in dark glasses and a blazer, a local who
instantly pegged us as out-of-towners.

"Ma, voi a chi partieni?" he asked, peering at us curiously.
To whom do you pertain? This remains one of the most wonderful ways I've ever been asked precisely what the hell I was doing
somewhere.

I was stunned by the directness of it, but that wasn't unfamiliar, either. My grandfather had had this same sort of way
about him, intrusive, charming, entirely unsubtle.

"My family was from here, but they left for America quite a
while ago," I said, before trailing off, expecting the conversation
to end there. But he continued to stare at me expectantly, and
I realized it would be rude not to divulge the answer to every
online security question I've ever been asked. So I began to tell

him my mother's name, and my grandparents', and he soon cut me off, nodding.

"Oh, of course," he said, as though he'd already known this fact and I'd just reminded him of it. He pointed down the hill from which he had come, explaining that my grandfather's sister had a house down there. I remembered this, vaguely, and was about to mention that fact, but he'd already taken off down the hill, beckoning us to follow.

"Come," he said, walking at a crisp clip in the sunlight. "I'll introduce you to some of your relatives."

I raced to follow him, and Rand, in turn, hurried to follow me, completely confused.

"Where are we going?" Rand asked.

"Um . . . to meet some of my relatives?" I'd forgotten, momentarily, that our conversation had been entirely in Italian and Rand had been unable to follow it. When I tried translating the exchange to English—tried explaining that we were following a stranger down a hill in a foreign town to meet more strangers—it made less and less sense. This felt like my family in microcosm.

"Who?"

"No idea."

A few minutes later the white-haired gentleman stopped at a little house made of white stone on a tranquil, sunlit street and promptly began banging on the front door while screaming, "OPEN UP, I'VE BROUGHT YOU YOUR RELATIVES."

This is not generally how I like to make an entrance. I prefer to stay away from any lines that could conceivably be uttered by an unstable character in a Scorsese film, particularly before 10 a.m. on a Sunday. The door opened, and a formidable-looking gentleman wearing a black tracksuit and an understandably pissed-off expression glared at us with piercing blue eyes.

"I've brought you your relatives," the white-haired man said again. Somehow—miraculously—he was already inside the house. "Invite them in."

Mr. Tracksuit's expression softened, but his bright blue eyes betrayed him: he had no idea who we were. He was fortyish and bald, not at all unhandsome, with a square jaw that was vaguely familiar to me. But then again, everything in the village was.

He introduced himself as Valerio, and, somewhat surprisingly, he did exactly as the white-haired man said and invited us in. His wife—wearing a pink tracksuit and sweetly greeting us with a kiss on either cheek even before it was clear who we were—put the espresso maker on the stove. Standing in the small house, I realized I'd been there before. I recognized the archways, the white walls, even the small room off to the left, where I remembered a photo of my great-grandfather had hung on the wall.

Our great-grandfather, as it turned out. We soon put the pieces together—my grandfather and Valerio's grandmother had been brother and sister.

"Right, right," he said, slapping an enormous hand down on the table, "the one who went to America."

"Wait, wait," his wife said from the kitchen, a glimmer of recognition flickering across her face. "Was he the one with the hair?" And she held her hands out on either side of her head.

I laughed. Yes. The hair.

My grandfather was one of the most stylish people who ever lived. In his healthier years, he wore a suit nearly every day, with some wide, quasi-psychedelic tie knotted in a full Windsor under a massive, stubbly chin.

In my parents' wedding album, there is a picture of my mother with her father that was perfectly emblematic of who he was. In it, the two of them are standing with the ruins of the Roman Forum behind them. My mother looks angelic in a simple floor-length dress, and my grandfather stands next to her in a dark three-piece suit and Persol sunglasses, looking cool as shit, as though the beautiful woman on his arm might be his youngest daughter, or possibly just his date for the night.

And yet despite this, and so many other singular characteristics (including the ability to crack walnuts open by simply squeezing them in his fist), the thing that nearly everyone remembers about him was his hair.

My grandfather had masses of it. If I search through my earliest memories, I can remember it being silvery gray, a rolling storm cloud above his head. But for most of my life it had the texture and color of raw wool.

He would take a wide-toothed comb and sweep it all forward, covering his eyes, and then comb it all back. Because there was no chance of it staying put, my grandfather would hold his hair in place with a thin plastic headband—the kind you could buy at the drugstore by the dozens in the 1970s and 1980s. My nonno would match the colors to his suits and ties. (If you are wondering whether you can pull this off, I can safely say this: unless you are my grandfather, then no. No, you cannot.)

Everyone, even people who barely knew my nonno, had stories about him. Some flattering, others not so much. He was generous to a fault; he was the life of the party; he had a temper; he yelled; he drank too much. I've heard everyone's tales of him, whether I've wanted to or not. I figure it's not fair to hold against him memories that are not my own. I try not to convict him by hearsay.

At my insistence, he would pick strawberries from his small garden and wash and cut them just for me. I single-handedly decimated those plants like a plague of locusts. When someone inquired as to what had become of the fruit, he would just shrug and say, "It's gone."

On Wednesdays and Sundays he would shave, working his shaving cream up into a lather with a badger hairbrush. He knew I loved this process, and so he let me sit and watch as he applied the foam all around his face and then shaved it off.

People have told me he was a jerk. I remember him letting me press my hands into his hair and squeeze it like a sponge. You love who you love; not everyone else has to.

We finished our coffee and a little while later left with the white-haired man. And there, on the street, after he led us down the hill and after he pounded on Valerio's door and after he invited us and himself in and after he shared his memories of my grandparents and after he drank an espresso, he *finally* saw fit to tell us his name: Marciano.

It was nearing lunchtime, and I'd unexpectedly found my grandfather's relatives but was still unsure where my grandmother's family lived. I realized that Marciano, who seemed to be a collector of stories that were not his own, might know where their house was.

"Via San Giovanni," he said. "Sempre su." *Always up.*

And so as he walked down the slope of the road, we walked up. We reached the top of the village, Rand warily asking me if I knew where I was going, and I offering uncomforting replies like "Maybe" or "No" or "The door is green." But the strange thing was, I never felt lost. I never made a wrong turn. I just kept walking, as though I knew the way.

Here, and absolutely no place else in the world, I knew where I was going.

Knowing the color of a building's door in lieu of its address is not generally useful when you are trying to locate it, and my tendency to retain useless information of that nature is part of the reason I'm consistently lost. But somehow, here, in my grandparents' village, knowing the color of the door was enough. There were at least half a dozen in varying shades of emerald, but I was able to pick out the right one. Massive, with an arched top, and centuries old.

We found my mother's cousin inside the courtyard, and eventually we'd all congregate there—my great-aunt, tiny and bright-eyed and animated with a sort of playfulness that was absent from her sweet, serious sister, my own dear grandmother. The two Ginos would arrive, as would my uncle and aunt and my green-eyed cousin, Valeria, who enters a room the way my mother does: like an affectionate hurricane, knocking over people and houseplants and load-bearing walls with an assault of hugs and kisses.

We sat around the table for several long hours. My family had given Rand the seat at the head of it, a place of honor usually reserved for some much older relative. I remembered all the *pranzos* of my childhood, my grandfather on one end of the table, my grandmother on the other.

In Italy, the midday meal of *pranzo* is a sort of sprawling feast, lasting hours. It is the reason many of the shops in Italy are closed between noon and 3 p.m. Because food is more important than capitalism.

In hindsight, I probably should have warned Rand.

"Pace yourself," I should have said.

Honestly, though, I thought he *knew*. That is why I didn't lean over and whisper, "There are four more courses to go."

I mean, why *else* are they called *primi* and *secondi*? They are referring to courses. What they don't really mention in Italian restaurants is that those are just the beginning.

There are also *antipasti* and *contorni* and *insalate* and *dolci*. There is wave after wave of food, eaten by ridiculously skinny people. (Don't ask me how this works, because I haven't cracked that part of the code. I can only assume that incorporating vigorous hand gestures into conversation burns crazy amounts of calories.)

When I was a kid, I would return home from school just as my grandparents were finishing up *pranzo*. There would be a massive white tablecloth on the table, decorated with breadcrumb confetti and the occasional stain of wine or pasta sauce, in dueling hues of red.

Since most of my family came to America right around the time I was born, those early memories in Seattle are of people who were far more mired in their Italian-ness than they are now. I remember my grandmother making pasta on a hand-cranked machine in the kitchen. Pigs' feet cooking in massive pots. A stovetop espresso maker that was constantly being forgotten on a burner.

But I was an American, with American friends and American habits, and so I soon learned that my family was not the norm. That other people didn't eat lunch for three hours while lovingly screaming at one another across a table. And as the years passed, my family would become more Americanized, too. Not enough to fit in, not enough to blend seamlessly, but enough.

The biggest meal of the day became dinner. Lunch became smaller. Pasta was exclusively of the dried variety, and sometimes it was cooked past *al dente*.

Things changed. But the foundation of all those meals of my childhood remained, and so the structure and timing of authentic Italian meals never was all that foreign to me. It's more like a rediscovered memory.

Rand carried with him the assumption that my family's habits in America were the same as they were in Italy. The multicourse extravaganza was more of a stereotype than actual practice. And so, when a massive plate of pasta was placed in front of him, the noodles hand-rolled by my aunt Rosamaria with a bit of help from her mother, he ate it with the (mis)understanding that this was the entirety of the meal. He even took a bit more when it was offered to him.

Rand is a notoriously slow eater, and as he finished the last bit of pasta, he looked up, trying to figure out why everyone was watching him so expectantly. And when he placed the last bite in his mouth, one of my uncles clapped and two or three people at the table shouted, "Finalmente."

Rand apologized for taking so long to finish, failing to understand what the big deal was. Weren't Italian meals hours-long affairs?

Yes. They undoubtedly are. But until he finished his pasta, we couldn't get on to the next course. That was what he didn't grasp.

The look on his face when my aunt brought the rest of the food out will remain etched in my memory forever. His jaw dropped, ever so slightly, his eyebrows knitting in the middle. And then he broke out into a small smile and a shaking of his head, as he finally realized what had happened.

He had stuffed himself on the first course. And there was so much more food to come.

The meats and sausages that had been stewed in tomato sauce. My aunt's *costolette di vitello* (tender slices of veal, breaded and fried). A place of vinegary vegetables that she'd pickled herself. A massive, simple green salad. A dish that resembled a frittata but was loaded with potatoes and pecorino and surprisingly little egg. An assortment of salumi and cheeses, most of which were made locally. They were placed on the table, along with the expectation that he would try a little bit of everything.

And, being the love of my life, he did just that.

When I asked him about it later, he told me that he just took a deep breath and thought, "Okay, let's move on to stomach number two."

We were at the table for hours. As we ate, my uncles and aunts affectionately shouted at each other across the table. My cousin gave Rand a highly biased (but still totally accurate) account of why food in southern Italy is far superior to the cuisine of the north. My great-aunt occasionally broke into the conversation with some declaration, her hands waving. Something about the cadence of her speech reminded me of my grandmother. And yet the closeness of their voices only made me think of the differences between them.

I participated in the conversation, but I kept having to stop, kept needing help on words or phrasing. When I finally did say something, or a long stretch of somethings, I'd pause and ask my cousin if I had said it right. I used to speak the language so well. When I was little, it was effortless.

For dessert, we dipped amaretti into red wine and nibbled on chocolates and talked about how we'd eaten too much.

After it was over, I looked at the tablecloth. We'd decorated it in the same manner that we had those of my childhood. With drops of wine and smears of bright red sauce, and a generous sprinkling of breadcrumbs.

I realized that this was what I had wanted Rand to experience. This was why I had dragged him all the way to a tiny village nestled in the mountains. I wasn't trying to show him Italy. I was trying to show him what my family was like when I was young. Back when lunch lasted three hours and I spoke Italian effortlessly and my grandparents weren't simply alive—they were *life*.

When I was small, I remember my grandmother talking to me about how I'd one day get married. I never put too much thought into it—the idea seemed distant and remote, and honestly, as the years passed, I'd never considered it an inevitability. In high school and college, I would sit and relay to her all the drama of my life (somewhat censored), would spend long hours telling her about who I was dating or who I had a crush on. She would nod, ask a few follow-up questions, and always conclude with, "If you're happy, then I'm happy."

She would meet every boyfriend I had until Rand. There is nothing I can do to change this unfortunate reality. There's no way for me to go back in time, to let her know that I would end up absurdly, ridiculously happy.

The closest I can come to that is to take him to the village where she and my grandfather lived, to crowd around a table with my family, eating too much and laughing too loudly for far too many hours.

Though seemingly interminable, that meal and that day came to an end. We said our goodbyes, long, drawn-out affairs that involved dozens of kisses and promises to visit more. We all dispersed, and Rand and I walked through the village in the fading light of day.

There, walking arm in arm with him on the streets where my grandparents once walked, I gave voice to the same thought I always had when I missed them acutely.

"I wish you'd met them," I said. It wasn't a particularly emotional or even sad admission. It was just the truth.

His answer was short and matter-of-fact.

"I sort of feel like I have."

And I realized that even though I'd spent earlier trips to this tiny village searching for my grandparents, this time around, I wasn't doing that. For the first time in a long time, they didn't feel so far away.

We walked back down the hill, I navigating the narrow streets of their village, arm in arm with a man they never knew, but who knew nearly everything about them that I could remember.

I never slowed down as I made my way back to our little bed and breakfast, never made a single wrong turn.

17

JUST GO

AS I'VE GOTTEN OLDER, I've noticed that there seem
to be fewer flight delays now than when I was a kid. I figured it
had to do with the patience that naturally comes with age, but I
recently found that's not the case. There really *are* fewer delays,
and flights get canceled far less often than they used to ten or
twenty years ago.

It's because airplane technology has gotten so good that the
pilots don't need ideal conditions to land or take off. Visibil-
ity isn't that important. Everyone I've relayed this fact to always
seems to think it's incredible—but it's not all that surprising to
me. Sometimes you can't see the path you're on. That doesn't
mean there isn't one.

I never imagined that putting more miles between myself
and the people closest to me would somehow help me understand them better than I ever had. That the chaos of Italy made
my mother less cryptic or that a clock in a distant corner of
Greenwich would help me understand my father. My brothers,

my cousins, my aunts and uncles, and my grandparents—I got lost on winding streets and in turn found myself deciphering all the people I thought I knew so well.

Sometimes in order to understand where someone is coming from, you need to *literally* see where that person came from.

And in the end the perfect trips I had with Rand were not the revelatory ones. It was all the mishaps—the missed turns and the overflowing toilets and the lost suitcases—that made me realize I'd follow him to the ends of the earth.

When I started my blog, all those years ago, I never thought it would take the place of the job I had lost. When I began traveling with Rand, I never suspected that I'd keep doing it, that somehow I—seemingly the least-qualified person on the planet to do so—would ever write a book about it.

In my defense (and you should know this by now), this book isn't going to teach anyone how to travel. The only thing this book can do, if you read very closely and critically, is teach someone how *not* to travel.

But I think there's value in that, too. Because travel writers are always weighing in on how we should see the world. That we all need to follow the road not taken, that we need to quit our jobs and sell all our stuff and buy quick-dry underwear that we wash nightly in our hostel sink. They tell us what to pack and which places to visit and how Cuba is just so *over* now that Americans can legally travel there.

Most of the time they use that damn J.R.R. Tolkien quote to tell you just how hardcore they are.

"Not all who wander are lost."

But you know what? I usually am. Hell, even if I'm not wandering, I'm lost. I might be striding down a street confidently, and to any observer it looks like I know exactly where I'm going. Believe me when I tell you I *don't*.

"Not all who are lost wander."

And that's okay. There are very few moments in our lives when we get to embrace sucking at something. When we get to fail miserably and still find value in it. Travel is one of those things. Even if you don't end up where you planned, you still might end up somewhere great.

ACKNOWLEDGMENTS

My friend Dan told me specifically not to thank people by name in the Acknowledgments section of your book, because you will inevitably forget someone critical. As a safeguard against this eventuality, I'd like to begin by offering thanks to this list of pet names I just came up with. I will kindly ask that any dear, overlooked friends pick the one that best applies to them:

> Little Frankenstein
> The Phantom of the Oprah
> Lady MacCheese
> Goatface Killah
> Old Tidy Bastard
> Gonad the Barbarian
> Other Dan
> Mike

Thank you all.

On a rare serious note, I am truly humbled by the amount of help, guidance, and support I have received in creating this work and would be remiss to not mention those wonderful souls who are to blame for making it a reality.

My perpetually positive and endlessly supportive agent, Zoe Sandler, believed in this project before I believed in it myself. Without her invaluable feedback, guidance, and expertise, I'd probably be . . . I don't know, supporting myself by kidnapping house pets and ransoming them back to their owners. You're the best, Zoe. No, you are.

My incredible editor, Colleen Lawrie, made this book funnier and more beautiful than I ever could have with her keen eye and amazing sense of humor. She displayed a bottomless reserve of patience and unparalleled professionalism while dealing with my incoherent asides and rambling phone calls, and she was surprisingly indulgent every time I wanted to talk about *Hamilton* and Daveed Diggs instead of narrative arcs. You had me at "Let's meet at a pastry shop," Colleen.

I am indebted to the entire team at PublicAffairs who helped bring this product into fruition, dealt with my incessant questions, my what-the-hell-was-I-talking-about-again emails, and patiently helped me with humor and grace: Jaime Leifer, Kristina Fazzalaro, Melissa Veronesi, Miguel Cervantes, and Lindsay Fradkoff.

A sincere thanks to my blog readers, for their support and their kind words and for being my personal curators for any news articles pertaining to desserts or Jeff Goldblum. Y'all are my favorite kind of weirdos.

I owe a great deal to my friend Kerry Colburn for her invaluable advice about publishing and life in general, as well as her willingness to meet me over baked goods. Kerry, if we all had the same confidence in ourselves that you have in us, we'd probably be locked in a bitter battle over dominion of Earth.

The luminous Emma Alpaugh was a constant source of support and wisdom and endless optimism and I kind of hope she agrees to run away with me someday.

Cristina Urrutia once took me to a bookstore and waved her arms around, saying, "Pssh, you got this," while simultaneously ignoring my self-deprecating ramblings. Happy, happy everything to you, Cristina.

Christina Atkins has made my life brighter simply by being in it. You are a wonderful human, Chrissy, and an incredible friend.

Nicelle Herron's hard work and thoughtfulness made so many of these trips possible and is the primary reason why Rand and I aren't useless lumps of human goo. We love you to pieces, Nicci.

Chad Peacock was the driving force behind me completing a manuscript in the first damn place. You are a royal pain in the ass, Chad. (Just look what you made me do.)

Many awkward hugs and thanks to my writer's group (which soon proved just a veiled excuse to eat carbohydrates)— Marika Malaea, Pam Mandel, and Naomi Bishop Tomky—for their humor, guidance, and encouragement. And all the cake.

Thank you to all our countless dear friends across the entire planet who have made us feel at home in far-off places and tried in vain to get us acclimated to the local time. You are a big part of why we travel. Sorry we fell asleep at the dinner table/in your car/on your toddler.

To everyone who's ever had the misfortune of traveling with us: sorry I freaked out that one time and that I haven't yet uploaded our vacation photos. Also, I think we owe you money. Or maybe you owe us money? If it's the latter, that's cool, take your time. I don't want stuff to get weird between us.

Much love and gratitude to Seymour and Pauline Fishkin for teaching their grandson how to read a map, ride the subway, and pick out the best theater seats for your dollar. He's got a hell of a tuchas on his shoulders, and it's all thanks to you.

My wonderful, crazy, inimitable family: thank you for giving me and my therapist so much to talk about. Thank you for reminding me that the world was always bigger than I thought it was and for never, ever being boring. (Note: you have not been absolved of anything.)

Lastly, endless thanks, praise, and apologies are owed to the undisputed love of my life, Rand Fishkin. Contrary to the implications of Chapter 2, you don't actually make a mess of the toilet, but you do laugh at all my terrible jokes and make me obnoxiously happy. I'd go the whole wide world just to find you.

Credit: Rand Fishkin

After getting laid off from her copywriting job, GERALDINE DeRuiter started traveling the world chronicling her adventures on her blog, The Everywhereist. Despite consisting mostly of long digressions about cake and Jeff Goldblum, the site was named one of *TIME* magazine's Top 25 Blogs of the Year, one of *Forbes* magazine's Top 10 Lifestyle Websites for Women for three consecutive years, and one of *The Independent*'s 50 Best Travel Websites. Also, she was once interviewed for a *US News & World Report* article about motion sickness (mostly, she talked about barfing).

When not on the road with her long-suffering and infinitely patient husband, Rand, she can be found in Seattle, usually getting into fights with people on the Internet. You can follow Geraldine on Twitter @everywhereist.